WRITERS AND THEIR WORK

ISOBEL ARMSTRONG
General Editor

SAMUEL JOHNSON

SAMUEL JOHNSON

SAMUEL JOHNSON

Liz Bellamy

© Copyright 2005 by Liz Bellamy

First published in 2005 by Northcote House Publishers Ltd, Horndon, Tavistock,
Devon, PL19 9NQ, United Kingdom.
Tel: +44 (01822) 810066. Fax: +44 (01822) 810034.

British Library Cataloguing-in-Publication Data
A catalogue record for this book is available from the British Library

ISBN 0-7463-1132-X hardcover
ISBN 0-7463-1131-1 paperback

Typeset by TW Typesetting, Plymouth, Devon

Printed and bound by CPI Group (UK) Ltd, Croydon, CR0 4YY

Contents

Preface

In recent years, two distinct images of Samuel Johnson have emerged from critical works. One is of a deeply conservative writer, upholding the literary tradition derived from the Greek and Latin classics and embodying residual ideology in his beliefs about politics, religion, and morality. The other is of a bold innovator, eagerly embracing new ideas and the new print technology. This short study will explore Johnson's major works in the light of these divergent views, and in the context of the changes that were taking place in the eighteenth-century literary world. It will indicate that Johnson's works need to be understood in the context of both the traditions of the past and the changes of the present. The development of Johnson's literary style should be seen as a reaction, but not necessarily a direct response, to the demands of the emergent readership.

Biographical Outline

1709	18 September: Samuel Johnson born in Lichfield, Staffordshire. Shortly after birth he contracted scrofula, a tubercular infection.
1717–25	Enters Lichfield Grammar School.
1725	Lives with his cousin, Reverend Cornelius Ford.
1725–6	Attends school in Stourbridge.
1726–8	Loiters at home in Lichfield, reading widely.
1728	Enters Pembroke College in Oxford University.
1729	December: Leaves Oxford without completing his degree. Returns to Lichfield. Suffers bout of severe depression.
1731	Father, Michael Johnson, dies.
1732	Works as usher in school in Market Bosworth, Leicestershire.
1733	Stays with Edmund Hector in Birmingham and dictates translation of Father Lobo's *Voyage to Abyssinia* while lying in bed.
1735	*Voyage* published. Marries Elizabeth Porter (Tetty). Establishes Edial Hall School.
1736–7	Works as schoolmaster and writes play, *Irene*.
1736	Leaves for London with David Garrick. Returns to Lichfield in Summer to finish *Irene*. Moves to London with Tetty.
1737	Writes for Cave's *Gentleman's Magazine*. Publishes parliamentary debates and *London*.
1739–44	Publishes political and biographical pieces, including *Life of Savage* (1744).
1745	*Miscellaneous Observations on the Tragedy of Macbeth* contains proposals for an edition of Shakespeare's plays.

1746	Begins work on *Dictionary* following approach from group of booksellers.
1747	*Plan for a Dictionary of the English Language.*
1749	*The Vanity of Human Wishes. Irene* performed at Drury Lane Theatre at the instigation of David Garrick. Runs for nine nights.
1750–2	Produces weekly *Rambler* essays.
1752	Wife Tetty dies.
1753	Contributes to *Adventurer*.
1755	Receives honorary degree from Oxford University. Writes famous *Letter to Chesterfield*. First edition of *Dictionary* published.
1756	Arrested for debt. Released after intervention from Samuel Richardson. Edits *Literary Magazine*. Second edition of *Dictionary* published.
1758–60	Weekly *Idler* essays.
1759	Mother, Sarah Johnson, dies. Publishes *Rasselas, Prince of Abyssinia*, to raise money to pay for funeral.
1762	Granted annual pension as recognition of literary achievements.
1763	Meets James Boswell.
1765	Edition of Shakespeare's plays published. Awarded honorary doctorate by Trinity College, Dublin.
1767	Meets George III while working in royal library.
1770–1	Publishes political pamphlets, *The False Alarm* and *Thoughts on the Late Transactions Respecting Falkland's Islands*.
1773	Tours Scotland with Boswell. Fourth edition of *Dictionary* published.
1774	Tour of Wales with Hester and Henry Thrale. First Collected Edition of Johnson's works published.
1775	Visits France with Thrales. Publishes *A Journey to the Western Islands of Scotland*.
1781	Publishes *Prefaces to the Works of the English Poets*. Henry Thrale dies.
1784	Johnson's intimate friend Hester Thrale marries Gabriel Piozzi, an Italian musician. Johnson is mortified and unable to hear her name mentioned. 13 December: Johnson dies. 20 December: Buried Westminster Abbey.

1785   James Boswell's *Journal of a Tour to the Hebrides* and William Shaw's *Memoirs of the Life and Writings of the Late Samuel Johnson* appear.

1786   *Anecdotes of the Late Samuel Johnson* by Mrs Piozzi (Hester Thrale) published.

1787   *Life of Samuel Johnson LLD* by Sir John Hawkins published.

1788   Hester Piozzi's *Letters to and from the late Samuel Johnson* published.

1791   James Boswell's *Life of Samuel Johnson, LL.D.* published

1795   James Boswell dies.

References and Abbreviations

The Yale edition of the *Works of Samuel Johnson* is a massive, multi-volume project providing an authoritative scholarly edition of Johnson's complete works. It has made an invaluable contribution to Johnson studies and represents the definitive version of the texts. It is, however, rather bulky and expensive and many readers will find it more convenient to use the single-volume paperback collection, *The Oxford Authors: Samuel Johnson*, ed. Donald Greene (Oxford, 1984). This includes most of the major poetry and prose works, substantial selections from the periodical literature, and extracts from the diaries and letters. References to prose works will be given to Greene, but where a work is not included in Greene, the reference will be to the Yale edition, giving volume and page number. All quotations from Johnson's poetry are taken from Greene's edition.

The following abbreviations are used.

DeMaria Robert DeMaria, Jr., *The Life of Samuel Johnson: A Critical Biography* (Oxford: Blackwell, 1993)

Greene *The Oxford Authors: Samuel Johnson*, ed. Donald Greene (Oxford: Oxford University Press, 1984)

Journal James Boswell, *Journal of a Tour to the Hebrides with Samuel Johnson, LLD*, The Yale Edition of the Private Papers of James Boswell, ed. Frederick Pottle and Charles Bennett (London: William Heinemann, 1961)

Life James Boswell, *The Life of Samuel Johnson*, ed. R. W. Chapman, rev. J. D. Fleeman, with an introduction by Pat Rogers (Oxford: Oxford University Press, 1980)

London   *London, A Poem in Imitation of Juvenal's Third Satire*

Vanity   *The Vanity of Human Wishes, The Tenth Satire of Juvenal Imitated*

Works   *The Yale Edition of The Works of Samuel Johnson,* General Editor, John H. Middendorf (New Haven and London: Yale University Press, 1958–)

Introduction

His person was large, robust, I may say approaching to the gigantic, and grown unwieldy from corpulency. His countenance was naturally of the cast of an ancient statue, but somewhat disfigured by the scars of that *evil*, which it was formerly imagined the *royal touch* could cure. ... He wore a full suit of plain brown clothes, with twisted hair buttons of the same colour, a large bushy greyish wig, a plain shirt, black worsted stockings and silver buckles. ... He wore boots, and a very wide brown cloth great coat, with pockets which might have almost held the two volumes of his folio dictionary; and he carried in his hand a large English oak stick. (*Journal*, 8)

James Boswell's description of Samuel Johnson in his sixty-forth year, about to embark on a tour of the Highlands of Scotland, conveys an idea of the huge physical stature and presence of the man. This, allied with Johnson's notorious and formidable intellectual power, has ensured that he is frequently described as a giant of English culture. He dominated the literary world of the eighteenth century, and has become an icon, the archetype of the professional man of letters. Yet it is customary to commence a study of Johnson with the paradoxical observation that this quintessential writer is now more read about than read. Most of us first encounter Johnson not through the pages of *Rasselas* or the *Rambler*, but through Boswell's lively biography. We know of his bons mots, his erudite conversation, and his crushing put-downs. Boswell's evocative portrait of genius battling against depression and psychological disturbance has become a definitive symbol of the struggling artistic soul. Our images of many eighteenth-century writers, such as Henry Fielding and Laurence Sterne, are largely derived from the works that they produced. Fielding is assimilated with the tolerant and genial narrator of *Tom Jones* and Sterne is identified with his comic creations, Tristram Shandy and Yorick. Yet with Johnson it is the other way round. We see the works in the light of our knowledge of the author and we impose our image of him upon them.

This book will analyse the works of Johnson in the context of the social and literary landscape of the eighteenth century, and one of its central concerns will be the issue of why these works are simultaneously so famous and so neglected. In part the answer lies in Boswell's biographical skill, which generated an image that was so powerful and resonant that it threatened to overwhelm the works. Part of the answer is in the strength of Johnson's personality and the general recognition, even in his own time, of his cultural significance. He was the subject of several biographical studies before Boswell's work was published, and the public appetite for anecdotes of his life was stimulated rather than satiated by William Shaw's *Memoirs of the Life and Writings of the Late Samuel Johnson*, published in 1785, the *Anecdotes of the Late Samuel Johnson* by Mrs Piozzi (formerly Hester Thrale) of 1786, and Sir John Hawkins's *Life of Samuel Johnson LLD* of 1787. But this is not the whole story. Johnson was working at a time of great upheaval in the literary establishment. Knowledge was becoming increasingly specialized, as subjects such as economics, politics, and moral philosophy began to develop their own distinct discourses, with their own vocabularies and terms of reference. At the same time, the emergence of a wider popular readership meant that the literary market was expanded and new forms of writing were developed to meet its needs. Johnson's œuvre, with its range of literary techniques and its use of both new and classical genres, embodies many of the changes taking place in the eighteenth century, and the tensions between the modern and the traditional approach. This book will argue that Johnson's works need to be read as part of a wider debate about the status and function of literature and its relationship to a readership that was identified as increasingly broad based. Johnson utilized different literary forms as his ideas about the role of the reader developed. Yet the extent to which Johnson embraced the changes in literature and society

2

has been the subject of considerable critical contention in recent years. Alvin Kernan has emphasized the importance of developments in printing technology in his book *Printing Technology, Letters and Samuel Johnson*. Kernan constructs an image of Johnson as a writer who enthusiastically exploited changing technology, and whose works were fundamentally shaped by his interaction with new methods for the production and distribution of literature. While eighteenth-century writers such as Richard Savage, Christopher Smart, Oliver Goldsmith, Thomas Chatterton, and James Macpherson are identified as ultimately backward-looking, 'Johnson alone chose to be openly a modern'.[1] More recently, John Cannon and J. C. D. Clark have produced separate studies of Johnson's politics. Cannon has developed Donald Greene's work of 1960, which questioned the traditional identification of Johnson as a reactionary Tory, and highlighted the radicalism of his early works in particular.[2] Cannon represents Johnson as a mixture of radical and conservative elements. He argues that: 'In a number of instances – on education, prison reform, or slavery – he was if anything ahead of his day. But, as a general proposition, Johnson's opinions were run of the mill, though expressed with a vigour and often a wit that were all his own.'[3] As a result, Cannon takes Johnson as an embodiment of public opinion in Hanoverian England. J. C. D. Clark has presented a rather different image of Johnson, highlighting his adherence to classical tradition and relating this to his political opinions, which are characterized as Tory and Jacobite, supporting the exiled Stuart monarchy, and therefore as more conservative than the dominant ethos of his age.[4]

In his authoritative critical biography, Robert DeMaria Jr. has steered a middle course. He identifies Johnson as a humanist, working within a European cultural context. While he stresses Johnson's knowledge of the book trade, he suggests that this was juxtaposed with distaste for the purely mercantile aspects of the business. DeMaria argues that Johnson developed a successful formula for the production of literary works that involved 'using existing printed material to produce new books, and at the same time to transmit essential, profoundly conventional wisdom' (DeMaria, 31).

3

This book will explore Johnson's works in the light of these divergent readings. It will analyse the extent to which the texts manifest impulses towards the classicism of the past and how far they look forward to the representational codes and discursive divides of the future. The linguistic tensions and generic uncertainties will be used to throw light on the wider changes in the literary establishment of which Johnson was both an engine and a mirror.

Any book on Johnson will inevitably draw on James Boswell's vast and magisterial *Life of Johnson*. This is such a colourful source that it is tempting to insert quotations at every point, and since its publication Johnson has tended to be seen through the lens of Boswell. It is important to remember that, however quotable or interesting, Boswell's biography, like its competitors, the *Life* of Sir John Hawkins and the *Anecdotes* of Mrs Piozzi, represents a particular reading of Johnson. Despite the air of intimacy that pervades Boswell's account of his relationship with the great man, they first met when Johnson was 54 years old. The description of Johnson's life preceding that point was based on letters, journal entries, and other papers, but also on Johnson's own reminiscences, and those of his friends, enemies, and acquaintances. The *Life* therefore represents Boswell's construction of Johnson, drawing quite heavily on Johnson's construction of himself. While Boswell's friendship with his mentor may have given him insights into his character, it also meant that he was unlikely to be an impartial judge. He declares that, even before the two men met, he had 'the highest reverence' for the author, derived from reading his works, 'which had grown up in my fancy into a kind of mysterious veneration' (*Life*, 272). Thus, despite its chronological closeness to its subject, his *Life* is as much a work of interpretation and construction as a piece of twenty-first-century Johnson criticism, and needs to be treated with equal caution and scepticism.

This caution is particularly necessary when using the *Life*, and the conversations cited within it, as a source for Johnson's political or religious opinions. One of the facets of Johnson's character that emerges from Boswell's account is his willingness to take up an argument, not from conviction, but from a desire to display his rhetorical skill. As Boswell comments after a lengthy account of Johnson's arguments on the superiority of the Roman Catholic religion to the Presbyterian:

'What he said is here accurately recorded. But it is not improbable that if one had taken the other side he might have reasoned differently' (*Life*, 424–6). This may be Boswell defending his hero from charges of popery, which the former would probably have resented more emphatically than the latter. Nonetheless it is clear that, while Johnson was a man of strong moral, political, and religious convictions, he was also deeply interested in language and rhetoric. He saw conversation as an opportunity to practise the science of persuasion, and his skill could be displayed more clearly when he weighed in on the side of the weaker cause. As Boswell comments in his *Journal of a Tour to the Hebrides*, 'he sometimes talked for victory' (*Journal*, 7).

Some scepticism may even be necessary in relation to Johnson's literary verdicts. Johnson famously praised a passage from Congreve's *Mourning Bride*, saying that he 'recollected none in Shakespeare equal to it' (*Life*, 412). These words have been taken by various Johnson scholars to support arguments about Johnson's critical perspective and his views on contemporary drama. Yet, as Walter Jackson Bate points out, Johnson subsequently made clear to Mrs Thrale that he made such comments in order to tease David Garrick, who was notorious for his love of Shakespeare.[5] While Johnson's admiration of Congreve was sincere, he was probably overstating his case and Boswell reports that he was duly 'diverted' with the 'enthusiastick jealousy' that his words provoked in Garrick.

Samuel Johnson was born in the city of Lichfield in Staffordshire on 7 September 1709 (OS) (18 September NS), the eldest son of elderly parents, his father being 52 and his mother 40 at the time of his birth. His father, Michael Johnson, was the son of a day labourer, but had received a charity school education and been apprenticed to a London stationer. At the age of 24 he had established himself in Lichfield as a bookseller and bookbinder, but the business was always financially insecure. Robert DeMaria has emphasized the significant influence of his father's occupation on young Samuel Johnson's life: 'Books were an important part of Johnson's surroundings all his life, and from an early age he knew a good deal about them, not only what was in them but how they were produced, what they were made of, how much they cost, and how they were distributed' (DeMaria, 3). But it is also important to remember that ultimately Michael Johnson was an unsuccessful bookseller. Johnson was brought up surrounded by books, but also aware of the dangers and difficulties of the marketplace, and the problems involved in the economic exploitation of literature. His remark to Boswell that 'No man but a blockhead ever wrote, except for money' (*Life*, 731) is frequently cited as evidence of Johnson's acceptance of the commercial aspects of eighteenth-century literary production. But Johnson's literary heroes were not writers for the modern market, but the poets of the classical past. He saw himself as part of an intellectual tradition continuing down the centuries.

As a baby, Johnson had contracted 'scrofula', supposedly from his wet nurse. This was a tubercular infection of the lymph glands and caused the loss of much of the sight of his left eye and some of the hearing of his left ear. The left side of his face was partly paralysed, and boils scarred his skin. He also developed a psychological disorder that meant that he was afflicted by nervous tics, obsessive gestures, and compulsive behaviours. Boswell describes:

> His anxious care to go out or in at a door or passage by a certain number of steps from a certain point, or at least so as that either his right or his left foot (I am not certain which) should constantly make the first actual movement when he came close to the door or passage. Thus I conjecture: for I have, upon innumerable occasions, observed him suddenly stop, and then seem to count his steps with a deep earnestness; and when he had neglected or gone wrong in this sort of magical movement, I have seen him go back again, put himself in a proper posture to begin the ceremony, and, having gone through it, break from his abstraction, walk briskly on, and join his companion. (*Life*, 342)

Moreover:

> While talking or even musing as he sat in his chair, he commonly held his head to one side towards his right shoulder, and shook it in a tremulous manner, moving his body backwards and forwards, and rubbing his left knee in the same direction, with the palm of his hand. In the intervals of articulating he made various sounds

with his mouth, sometimes as if ruminating, or what is called chewing the cud, sometimes giving a half whistle, sometimes making his tongue play backwards from the roof of his mouth, as if clucking like a hen, and sometimes protruding it against his upper gums in front, as if pronouncing quickly under his breath, TOO, TOO, TOO. (*Life*, 343)

This pattern of symptoms has been retrospectively diagnosed as Tourette's Syndrome, an inherited neurological disorder that is characterized by repeated involuntary movements and uncontrollable vocal sounds. Some critics have suggested that this disorder may also have been the source of Johnson's extraordinary verbal and vocal power, but it was probably also connected with the recurrent bouts of depression that afflicted him for sustained periods during his life.

In 1728 Johnson became a student at Pembroke College, Oxford, after his mother inherited a small sum of money. On his arrival, he impressed his tutors with his knowledge of obscure classical texts, but, while he continued to read extensively, Johnson does not appear to have been a very conscientious student. Throughout his life he was afflicted by a combination of idleness and guilt. He would lounge in bed, unable to get up, yet mortified with anxiety at his failure to do so. This may have been another symptom of depression, and one against which Johnson struggled, largely unsuccessfully, throughout his life. Many of the notes and memoranda composed by Johnson that have been collected together as the *Prayers and Meditations* address this characteristic. For instance, in October 1729 Johnson recorded in Latin: 'I bid farewell to Sloth, being resolved not to listen to her syren strains.' Thirty-five years later, on 21 April 1764, he is still writing in a similar vein, commenting that: 'My indolence, since my last reception of the Sacrament, has sunk into grosser sluggishness. . . . My purpose is from this time To reject or expel sensual images, and idle thoughts. To provide some useful amusement for leisure time. To avoid Idleness. To rise early.'

When Johnson returned to Lichfield for Christmas in 1729 he found that his father was ill, and his financial affairs in chaos. This seems to have triggered Johnson's own depressive illness, and the combination of economic and physical factors ensured that he was unable to return to Oxford to complete his degree.

Following his father's death in 1731, Johnson sought to support himself by working as a teacher, and subsequently through writing and translating scholarly works. In July 1735, after another period of profound depression and inactivity, he married Elizabeth Porter (Tetty), to the great surprise of the friends and family of each. Johnson was then 25; she was a widow of 46. Despite widespread reports of their incompatibility and marital disharmony, despite frequent enforced separations, and his wife's addiction to drugs and alcohol in later years, Johnson always claimed that the marriage was a love match, and he was overcome with despair when Tetty died in 1752. Although he subsequently considered marrying again (Greene, 775), this never happened. For the rest of his life he composed prayers and spiritual reflections on his wife, solemnly commemorating her birthday and the day of her death, and these works exhibit a potent combination of affection, grief, and guilt for his failures as a husband.

Following his marriage, Johnson used the £600 brought to him by his wife to set up his own school at Edial outside Lichfield. This enterprise was not a success, due perhaps in part to Johnson's unprepossessing physical appearance and strange mannerisms. This was a period when parents sent their boys to school to learn the manners and deportment of a gentleman, rather than simply to acquire academic knowledge, and this was a branch of study Johnson was peculiarly unfitted to convey. His first biographer, William Shaw, suggests that:

> Parents could not be very fond of putting their children under the care of a man whose size was gigantic, whose temper was arrogant and austere, and whose habits were all clumsy and rude. His mind was as destitute of accommodation as his exterior was of politeness or grace; and to those who estimate genius or worth only by a soft tongue, a smooth face, or ceremonious carriage, his wit would appear insolence, his honesty folly, and his learning pedantry.[6]

He never had more than a handful of students, and the establishment closed in February 1737. By this time, Johnson had probably recognized that his most likely means of making sufficient money to support himself, his wife, and his elderly mother was through literature. He would have to become a professional writer, and the only place to do so at this time was

London. Thus on 2 March 1737 Johnson set out for London, accompanied by David Garrick, a former pupil from his academy, who was later to become the most famous and successful actor of the eighteenth century. The stories Garrick and Johnson told in subsequent years of this expedition, and of how they made this journey on foot with only four pence between them, are almost certainly apocryphal. Yet it is clear that both men, as they set out, had their fortunes to make and their reputations to establish.

In his pocket Johnson carried the manuscript of a play, *Irene*, which he may have thought would help in the process. It has an exotic Turkish setting, but it is classical in both its subject matter and its form. It is a formal verse tragedy, presenting a moral tale of spiritual faith and constancy, deceit and apostasy, with the good rewarded and the frail punished. In contrast to Johnson's later works, it was slowly and carefully written and painstakingly revised over a period of years, but it did not succeed in making either the names or the fortunes of the friends on their arrival in London. In fact, it was performed only in 1749, when Garrick had become established as a central figure in the London theatrical world and arranged to have it produced at Drury Lane as a favour to his impoverished friend. It appeared in print shortly afterwards, but it was not a critical success on either stage or page. Readers and audiences alike recognized the morality of the piece and the strength of its verse, but it was felt to be static and undramatic. One critic commented that 'the very soul of Tragedy, *Pathos*, is wanting; and without that, though we may admire our hearts will sleep in our bosoms'.[7] Another claimed 'so languid and unaffecting is this poem, that I very much question, if one maudlin girl squeez'd out a single tear, either at the theatre, or in the closet'.[8] William Shaw's account highlighted the inapplicability of Johnson's classical and moral form for a contemporary audience:

> The plot ... the thoughts, and the diction of his tragedy are allowed to be beautiful and masterly. But he is sparing of that bustle and incident, which atone for the want of every excellence with a London audience. A performance which exemplified the prescriptions of an Aristotle, was not likely to please a nation tutored in this barbarous taste.[9]

9

On his arrival in London Johnson turned to the publisher Edward Cave as a source of financial support, proposing various projects of translation and scholarly study and offering contributions for Cave's periodical *The Gentleman's Magazine*. Established in 1731, this was a more respectable production than its satirical and often scurrilous rival *The Grub-Street Journal*, and held out the possibility of a literary career that was compatible with the status of a gentleman.[10] Cave accepted a number of pieces of poetry on various subjects, and it was as a poet that Johnson first began to achieve literary success and some degree of critical acclaim.

1

London and *The Vanity of Human Wishes*

Throughout his life, from his youth as a schoolboy in Lichfield and Stourbridge to the final lingering days of decay following his stroke in 1783, Johnson occupied himself with the composition of verse. He wrote in both English and Latin and in a range of literary genres. His productions included light-hearted occasional verses addressed to his friends, prayers and spiritual meditations, tragedies, translations, odes, and epitaphs. Some was for publication but much for private consolation and the exploration of fears, doubts, and uncertainties. His tone was often satirical, as exemplified in his 'Parodies of Modern Ballad "Imitations" '. This mocked the growing vogue for poetry based on the simple verse form and everyday content of the newly popularized ballad tradition, and contained quatrains such as:

> I therefore pray thee, Renny dear
> That thou wilt give to me,
> With cream and sugar softened well,
> Another dish of tea.

> (Greene, 25)

On other occasions the tone was full of humanity, and he could touch a vein of pathos, as in his epitaph on the talented but impecunious musician, Claudy Phillips:

> Phillips! Whose touch harmonious could remove
> The pangs of guilty power, and hapless love,
> Rest here, distressed by poverty no more,
> Find here that calm thou gav'st so oft before;

11

Sleep undisturbed within this peaceful shrine,
Till angels wake thee with a note like thine.

(Greene, 9)

The two poems by Johnson that are most often read today are *London* and *The Vanity of Human Wishes*. These deal with contemporary moral and social issues, but they take the form of adaptations of works by the Roman satirist Juvenal. The genre of the Imitation has been little used since the early nineteenth century. Romantic poets such as Wordsworth, Coleridge, Byron, and Shelley had popularized the concept of poetry as a product of inspiration. The poet was a genius, wandering lonely as a cloud, waiting to be struck by the divine fire that would give birth to a work that could present the world in a new and original way. In the seventeenth century, and for most of the eighteenth, however, the image of the poet was rather different. He was a scholar rather than a child of nature, and composition was a consequence of knowledge and careful study. J. C. D. Clark has emphasized the significance of the classical tradition to all forms of writing in English in the early eighteenth century. He argues that the literary culture in which Johnson grew to maturity was a vernacular culture, in that it was largely written in English, 'but it was a vernacular culture which had developed in an intimate relationship with the classics'.[1] He suggests that the modern failure to appreciate Johnson's literary significance may in part be a consequence of the decline of classical knowledge.[2] We cannot see these works as part of a continuing tradition because we no longer pick up on the references and resonances that signal both connections and dissonances between the present and the past.

The dominance of Romantic images of the role and function of the poet has meant that our culture does not tend to value works that draw directly on other works. Ideas of poetic value have become inextricably tied to the concept of originality, and it takes an effort of historical imagination to recognize that this was not the case at the time when Johnson was writing. Up to the end of the eighteenth century, imitation was a highly respectable literary form. Between 1660 and 1700 at least fifty poets produced English translations of works by Horace alone, and thereafter the form became even more popular.[3] In a translation, the poet could display his (occasionally her) classical knowledge and virtuosity in the skill with which the Greek or Roman text was adapted to suit a contemporary context. Moreover, the writers could appeal to an elite readership, which could be assumed to have the requisite classical knowledge to get the full significance of the adaptation. In his 'Preface' to *Ovid's Epistles translated by Several Hands* (1680), John Dryden distinguished between three types of translation that he termed metaphrase, paraphrase, and imitation. Metaphrase was the most literal. It conveyed the direct meaning of the words of the original, but in doing so often failed to catch the spirit. Paraphrase retained the sense of the original, but without strict literalness, while imitation departed freely from the text to create a new poem, using the experience of a new age to take the place of earlier material.[4] In his 'Preface to Troilus and Cressida, containing the Grounds of Criticism in Tragedy' (1679), Dryden cites Longinus to provide a trenchant defence of this form of poetic composition:

> We ought not to regard a good imitation as a theft, but as a beautiful idea of him who undertakes to imitate, by forming himself on the invention and the work of another man; for he enters into the lists like a new wrestler, to dispute the prize with the former champion. ... Those great men, whom we propose to ourselves as patterns of our imitation, serve us as a torch, which is lifted up before us, as high as the conception we have of our author's genius.[5]

Dryden's words convey the optimism that underlay the neoclassicism of the late seventeenth and early eighteenth century. They are founded in a belief that the current age can be equated with the cultural peaks of the classical past, and that its genius can best be displayed by direct engagement with that past. Imitation is both in competition with the original, and a tribute to it, and Johnson's *London* is squarely within this dominant neoclassical tradition. In a letter to the bookseller Edward Cave, Johnson emphasized the need to have the original printed at the bottom of the page, 'part of the beauty of the performance ... consisting in adapting Juvenal's sentiments to modern facts and persons'.[6]

Towards the end of his life, Johnson celebrated Dryden's role in fixing 'the limits of poetical liberty' by creating 'just rules and examples of translation' in his essay on Dryden for the *Prefaces to the Works of the English Poets*. He stresses the problems and inadequacies of literal translation, arguing that:

> All polished languages have different styles: the concise, the diffuse, the lofty, and the humble. In the proper choice of style consists the resemblance which Dryden principally exacts from the translator. He is to exhibit his author's thoughts in such a dress of diction as the author would have given them, had his language been English. (Greene, 723–4)

Robert DeMaria has connected Johnson's use of the 'imitation' with his desire to construct a career and reputation based on scholarly and classical learning, rather than writing for a popular audience: 'Johnson shows his readers a way of interpreting Juvenal that displays his awareness of classical scholarship and his acute perception of Latin phraseology. Although he wrote it in English, Johnson was still proving his worth as a Latin poet and scholar in *London*' (DeMaria, 49).

LONDON

London came out shortly after Johnson settled in the city, and for it the publisher Robert Dodsley paid the substantial sum of ten guineas (*Life*, 91).[7] The poem uses Juvenal's third satire as a 'pattern of imitation', and, where Juvenal attacked the corruption that he observed in Rome in the second century AD, Johnson identified the same degeneration in eighteenth-century London. In each poem, a friend of the narrator explains why he is leaving the city for a life in the countryside, drawing on the traditional opposition of the country and the city. In places Johnson's verse is fairly close to the original, almost representing Dryden's category of paraphrase rather than the looser imitation. For example, in Juvenal's poem we are warned that:

> You'll be thought most improvident,
> A catastrophe-happy fool, if you don't make your will before
> Venturing out to dinner.   275
> .   .   .   .   .   .
> There's the drunken bully, in an agonised state

14

For lack of a victim, who lies there tossing and turning   280
The whole night through . . .
This lout is doomed to insomnia
Unless he gets a fight. Yet however flown with wine
Our young hothead may be, he carefully keeps his distance
From the man in a scarlet cloak, the man surrounded   285
By torches and big brass lamps and a numerous bodyguard.[8]

This is rendered by Johnson as:

Prepare for death, if here at night you roam,
And sign your will before you sup from home.   225
Some fiery fop, with new commission vain,
Who sleeps on brambles till he kills his man;
Some frolic drunkard, reeling from a feast,
Provokes a broil, and stabs you for a jest.
Yet ev'n these heroes, mischievously gay,   230
Lords of the street, and terrors of the way,
Flushed as they are with folly, youth, and wine,
Their prudent insults to the poor confine;
Afar they mark the flambeau's bright approach,
And shun the shining train and golden coach.   235

                              (*London*, ll. 224–35)

Elsewhere the translation is looser, an imitation rather than a paraphrase, as Johnson adapts Juvenal's original to expatiate on contemporary politics. Both Rome and London are presented as places where honest merit and industry go unrecognized, and hypocrisy, sycophancy, and criminality receive rich rewards. While the countryside is characterized as a haven of health and happiness, where the good man can find peace and recognition, the city is dangerous and inherently unstable: 'Here malice, rapine, accident, conspire, | And now a rabble rages, now a fire' (*London*, ll. 13–14). Juvenal's Rome has been corrupted by an influx of Greeks; Johnson's xenophobia is directed towards the French. In each poem, the foreigners are portrayed as servile and effeminate. They prosper through their willingness to flatter and pander to the whims of their superiors, while the native people suffer for their rugged honesty and truculent independence.

    Many critics have highlighted the irony of Johnson's authorship of this poem, given his renowned enthusiasm for the metropolis, encapsulated in the famous statement to Boswell that 'when a man is tired of London, he is tired of life' (*Life*, 859).[9] But the poem was not written, and would not have been read, as a statement of private, personal sentiments. It was an exercise in public, political rhetoric. The London from which Johnson's character Thales retreats is constructed as a Whig edifice, oppressed by taxation and overcome by luxurious decadence, depravity, and dissimulation. Johnson contrasts a Golden Age of national strength and integrity, which he locates in the Elizabethan era, with the corruption of the present. The modern age is symbolized by the popular festivity of the masquerade or masked ball, in which guests concealed their identities behind elaborate disguises that facilitated sexual misconduct. These events were generally associated with gambling and other forms of immorality and impropriety, and embodied the extravagance, the decadence, and the debauchery that were seen to characterize the conduct of the social elite (*London*, l. 29). Johnson represents a city that has declined from imperial glory and gives point to his satire by references to contemporary incidents that are seen to represent British decline. He refers to the attacks on British shipping by Spanish coast guards (*London*, l. 30), the licensing act (*London*, l. 59) and the imposition of taxes by the Committee of Ways and Means (*London*, l. 245). Howard Weinbrot highlights the nationalistic impulse behind this critique, suggesting that the poem 'regards the collapse of London as an emblem of the larger collapse of the nation'. Johnson 'laments French influence and British political decay, and portrays its speaker . . . as having to vacate the morally un-British city'.[10] He sees this assault on the government of Robert Walpole as part of a youthful flirtation with opposition politics that was rejected by Johnson in later life. This echoes the reading of Boswell, who uses the account of the poem in the *Life* to provide his own eulogy of Walpole as 'a wise and a benevolent minister', of whom, he claims, 'Johnson himself afterwards honestly acknowledged the merit'. *London* was, according to Boswell, a 'juvenile poem' that 'was naturally impregnated with the fire of opposition' (*Life*, 94).

Robert DeMaria identifies the attack on Walpole with Johnson's desire to protect the rights and privileges of his 'patron', the publisher Edward Cave, on the grounds that 'much of what Johnson deplores pertains to government intrusions into printing, publishing, and other aspects of the book trade that were affected by Walpole's general economic policies'. For DeMaria the poem is not a general critique of government, its attitude to trade and consumption and its relations with foreign powers. Rather 'it is for Johnson another act of professional identification, mixing non-feudal fealty to a patron with modern class and trade loyalty' (DeMaria, p. 51). This is Johnson as the hero of print culture, defending his trade against attack, yet this seems to put a rather parochial private interpretation on a poem that explicitly engages with a range of public political issues and locates itself within the partisan tradition of Juvenal.

Howard Erskine Hill and J. C. D. Clark have both seen a wider political relevance in *London*. They argue that the poem displays Johnson's sympathies with the Jacobite cause of the Stuart monarchy. The main evidence for this account is the identification of Thales with Johnson's friend Richard Savage, a dissolute writer who had previously expressed his support for the Jacobites.[11] If Thales is Savage, then the poem must endorse the views with which Savage was associated. Yet John Cannon has contested this claim, arguing that Savage had distanced himself from the Stuart cause and was seeking to ingratiate himself with Robert Walpole's administration by the time the poem was composed.[12] But, as Lawrence Lipking has pointed out, Savage and Johnson may not have met by the time of the poem's composition.[13]

It is clear that this kind of external evidence for Johnson's political stance is at best equivocal. We should not accept without question Boswell's assertion that Johnson's views underwent radical transformation so as to coincide with his own, and we cannot assume that, if Savage was used as the model for Thales, this necessarily meant that his current political views were echoed within the poem. Yet, as these conflicting interpretations reveal, the poem exemplifies the complexity of political affiliations and language in the first half of the eighteenth century, and the slippery nature of rhetoric and imagery that can be read as both radical and conservative.

The poem invokes the idea of a Golden Age of English liberty (*London*, ll. 248–51), when the country was characterized by honesty, justice, and independence. This rhetoric draws on the 'myth of the Norman yoke', the belief that the country was free and happy until the Norman Conquest in 1066 brought tyranny and rule by a corrupt aristocracy. This myth was particularly potent amongst the opposition parties in the first half of the eighteenth century, because it invited parallels between the Norman barons and the powerful political magnates of the day. After the accession of the Hanoverian George I in 1714 the parallel became particularly striking, since the aristocracy could be represented as the henchmen of another foreign monarchy.

This celebration of an era of liberty and justice was to become part of the radical rhetoric of the late eighteenth and nineteenth centuries, but here it is part of a different political tradition. Johnson combines this evocation of a rosy distant past with references to a glorious more recent past in the age of Elizabeth (*London*, ll. 23–8). This nostalgia gives force to the critique of the present, with its condemnation of the corruption of 'pension' (*London*, ll. 51, 73, 200) and its celebration of 'rights' (*London*, l. 53), 'Justice' (*London*, l. 250) and 'virtue' (*London*, l. 262)

This was the language of the Tory or Old Whig interest, generated in opposition to the Whig magnates who dominated the political system and monopolized political power from the death of Queen Anne in 1714. Some twentieth-century commentators have seen this language as part of a wider ideological framework that they have labelled 'Country Party', in contrast to the 'Court Party' of the Whig interest. Although in later life Johnson became a supporter of the government of Lord Bute, his personal beliefs remained staunchly Tory, drawing on the rhetoric of the Country Party tradition. They were characterized by a humanitarian concern for a perceived increase in poverty and the growing disparity between rich and poor; an opposition to government corruption and the increasing power of the executive; and a defence of British justice and liberty. These beliefs were already inscribed in the 'juvenile poem' *London*.

If considered in the light of the eighteenth-century ideological landscape, Johnson's political views seem far less anomalous and contradictory than they appear today. His condemnation of slavery reflects his human compassion, but it also fits in with his suspicion of trade and its increasing influence within the political system. The traffic in human life symbolizes the heartless acquisitiveness that is taken to characterize trade as a whole. Johnson's antagonism to slavery therefore needs to be seen, not as part of some radical agenda, anticipating developments later in the century, but as a consequence of a traditionalist opposition to economic expansion and to new forms of wealth.

THE VANITY OF HUMAN WISHES

The Vanity of Human Wishes was the first of Johnson's works to be published under his own name. It has been regarded by critics, from Boswell ('it is, in the opinion of the best judges, as high an effort of ethick poetry as any language can shew (*Life*, 139)) to Howard Weinbrot, as 'one of the great poems in the English language',[14] although David Garrick is said to have pronounced it 'as hard as Greek' (*Life*, 138). It is a moral rather than a political satire, with what Boswell describes as 'less of common life, but more of a philosophick dignity than . . . *London*' (*Life*, 138). The poem draws on the tenth satire of Juvenal, which explores the futility of human desires for wealth, fame, power, eloquence, glory, long life, and good looks. But Johnson combines the moral philosophy of the original with a meditation on the passage from Ecclesiastes in the Old Testament:

> Vanity of vanities, saith the Preacher, vanity of vanities; all *is* vanity.
> What profit hath a man of all his labour which he taketh under the sun?[15]

This meditation draws on a book that Johnson had first read when he was a student at Oxford, William Law's *Serious Call to a Devout and Holy Life* (1729). The Reverend Doctor Maxwell, in a memoir incorporated in Boswell's *Life*, records that Johnson described this as 'the finest piece of hortatory theology in any language' (*Life*, 440), and claimed that reading the book 'was the first occasion of [his] thinking in earnest of religion'

(*Life*, 50). Law draws on Ecclesiastes, to show the emptiness of human aspirations, and to demonstrate that fulfilment can be achieved only through religion.[16]

The Vanity of Human Wishes therefore combines the classical satire of Juvenal with the Christian theology of Law, to present a series of cameos that can inform a contemporary audience. The reader is invited to witness the rise of various great individuals, their success, and subsequent decline and failure. Abstract ideas such as power, wealth, military glory, or learning are personified, as in the famous portraits of Cardinal Wolsey (*Vanity*, ll. 99–128) or Charles XII of Sweden (*Vanity*, ll. 191–222), so that the reader can evaluate moral issues through reference to specific individuals. This was a method frequently employed in the poetry of Alexander Pope, where named characters embody vices such as avarice, prodigality, lack of taste, or lack of sense. It was also becoming increasingly important in the emerging novel form. Writers such as Samuel Richardson, Henry Fielding, and Eliza Haywood used the stories of particular individuals to exemplify a moral message, or to make moral points by showing the ethical development of the heroes and heroines in the course of their fictional experiences. This technique can be read as a means of making moral philosophy, or at least moral issues, accessible to a readership that would not have been equipped to handle the complex epistemology of works such as David Hume's *Treatise on Human Nature* (1739–40).

Johnson's poetry does not simply embody the abstract in the concrete, however. The language makes repeated shifts in register, so that the personified characters are themselves frequently portrayed figuratively. Pyrotechnic imagery in particular pervades the verse, inspired, perhaps, by the notorious failure of the spectacular firework show planned to celebrate the end of the War of Austrian Succession in April 1749.[17] The great are compared to fireworks – spectacular but transitory. The reader is shown various examples of how 'They mount, they shine, evaporate, and fall' (*Vanity*, l. 76) and the poem is replete with references to the processes of ascent, combustion, and descent. This is a metaphor that recurs in Johnson's writing. In the final *Rambler* (208), he refers to how he has seen 'the meteors of fashion rise and fall, without any attempt to add a moment to their duration' (*Works*, v. 316). This image of a comet or firework seems to encapsulate Johnson's belief in the transience and emptiness of human desires and achievements.

Howard Weinbrot has drawn attention to Johnson's use of verbs in his poetry,[18] and in the opening lines of *Vanity* we are exhorted, in a series of imperatives, to 'Remark', 'watch' and 'say' (*Vanity*, ll. 3–5). This reinforces the idea conveyed in the opening couplet:

> Let observation with extensive view,
> Survey mankind, from China to Peru.

> (*Vanity*, ll. 1–2)

Johnson suggests that we can learn from observation of mankind in general and that experience of the world and knowledge of the past can convey moral lessons. We are invited to use the portraits to reflect on human aspirations, but the conclusions we are expected to reach are significantly different from those of Juvenal's satire. Juvenal ends his series of portraits with the words:

> There's one
> Path, and one only, to a life of peace – through virtue.
> Fortune has no divinity, could we but see it: it's we,
> We ourselves, who make her a goddess, and set her in the
> heavens.[19]

For Johnson, this view that we make our own luck, and that our only true course in life is the pursuit of virtue, is converted into a frightening image of human isolation in an uncaring universe:

> Must helpless man, in ignorance sedate,
> Roll darkling down the torrent of his fate?

> (*Vanity*, ll. 345–6)

But the answer he gives to this question is an emphatic negative. *Vanity* ends with an assertion of faith in divine justice. Instead of relying solely on human virtue, as the 'path to peace', we should accept the role assigned to us by God. We may 'still raise for good the supplicating voice' but we must 'leave to heaven the measure and the choice' (*Vanity*, ll. 351–2).

21

We must perform good deeds and practise virtue, but assume that the reward for these actions will come not on earth but in heaven. It is up to God to determine its nature and extent. In a significant metaphoric elision, the image of the firework of human aspiration of the early section of the poem (*Vanity*, l. 76) is supplanted by an image of faith as a rocket shooting towards heaven:

> When the sense of sacred presence fires,
> And strong devotion to the skies aspires,
> Pour forth thy fervours for a healthful mind,
> Obedient passions, and a will resigned.

> (*Vanity*, ll. 357–60)

It is only through prayer and resignation that we can hope to obtain those 'goods' that Johnson presents as essential for tranquillity: mental health, acceptance, love, patience, and faith. The final couplet suggests some revision of the implied empiricism of the opening couplet. While we were initially exhorted to 'Survey mankind', the closing lines argue that this will not, in itself, give access to happiness. With reference to the 'goods', we are informed that:

> With these celestial wisdom calms the mind,
> And makes the happiness she does not find.

> (*Vanity*, 366–7)

While Johnson's verse has been directed to the human mind, and our minds have been encouraged to learn from the examples set before us, it is clear from this couplet that this endeavour will ultimately prove futile. She, the mind, will not be able to find happiness by herself. The firework of human aspiration will burn itself up, unless it is used to send an appeal up to heaven. The human spark pales into insignificance in contrast to the divine fire, which alone can convey happiness.

The close of the poem subverts the empiricist ideology of the opening, but also departs from the message of Juvenal's original. This would have been evident to the majority of Johnson's contemporary readers, who would have been well versed in classical scholarship and would have seen the poem as both a tribute to the classical era and a celebration of the ethical superiority of the modern Christian state. It could be read and enjoyed by readers with no knowledge of the original, but some aspects of its meaning and significance would inevitably be lost.

Despite the recent emphasis on Johnson as a modern writer, the embodiment of a new age of print technology and commerce,[20] these early Imitations suggest that, at least in the early years, Johnson was more of a transitional figure. He was anxious to exploit the economic potential of new technology, expand the market for books, and increase the income of authors. But he was also a writer who was immersed in the classics, and who could both write and speak in Latin with almost as much ease as in English. David Nichol Smith argues that Latin 'was the language which he preferred for the expression of certain moods and feelings'[21] and Howard Weinbrot suggests that it 'allowed him to hide sensitive thoughts from some others while exploring those thoughts himself'.[22] These quotations suggest a desire to exploit the exclusivity of language, as well as its inclusive potential. The genre of the Imitation epitomizes this, in that it implies a hierarchy of reading, in which those with classical knowledge are able to obtain a higher understanding than those without.

In later life, Johnson seems to have developed a more inclusive concept of reading, for in his *Life of Pope* he condemns the genre of the Imitation, in part on the grounds of its exclusivity:

> Such imitations cannot give pleasure to common readers. The man of learning may be sometimes surprised and delighted by an unexpected parallel; but the comparison requires knowledge of the original, which will likewise often detect strained applications. Between Roman images and English manners there will be an irreconcileable dissimilitude, and the work will be generally uncouth, and parti-coloured; neither original nor translated, neither ancient nor modern. (Greene, 750)

The Vanity of Human Wishes, however, draws much of its power from the creative exploitation of this 'irreconcileable dissimilitude', in that it highlights the tension between the ethical thinking derived from classical sources and Christian theology. It is clear that, however his views may have subsequently changed, at the time of the composition of these early poems, Johnson was happy to be working within a classical tradition and addressing himself to 'the man of learning'. As J. C. D. Clark explains, at the time of the composition of *London* and *The Vanity of Human Wishes*: 'To edit or translate a classical author was still to work within a living tradition; to write an "imitation" of a classical work was to appropriate that tradition by technical mastery of it, to give it renewed articulation, and to enlist the force and authority of a classic, behind one's own statements.'[23]

In the introduction to volume iii of the Yale edition of the *Works*, W. J. Bate and Albrecht B. Strauss argue that 'the great moral writing of the following decade, which begins with the *Rambler* and ends with *Rasselas*, may be described as the prose explication of the *Vanity of Human Wishes*' (*Works*, iii, p. xxviii). This may be true in respect of the moral themes explored in these works, but the 1750s saw a slight but discernible shift in Johnson's concept of the audience of literary works, and of the relationship between the text and the reader.

2

The *Rambler* and the *Idler*

From Tuesday, 20 March 1750 to Saturday, 14 March 1752 Johnson produced a regular twice weekly periodical entitled the *Rambler*. This was not like a modern magazine, which contains a range of articles by different people. Each *Rambler* addressed a particular topic, such as 'A Londoner's visit to the Country' (*Rambler* 61) or 'The Importance of Punctuality' (*Rambler* 201), and, with the exception of a handful of papers that are thought to have been wholly or partly supplied by friends, they were written by Johnson alone.[1] In this enterprise he followed in the steps of Richard Steele and Joseph Addison. In the early years of the century, the *Tatler* and *Spectator*, produced by Addison, Steele, and a group of friends, had established the pattern of the periodical essay. In his portrait of Addison in the *Prefaces to the Works of the English Poets*, Johnson paid tribute to these works. He argues that before these works were published

> England had no masters of common life. No writer had yet undertaken to reform either the savageness of neglect or the impertinence of civility. . . . We had many books to teach us our more important duties, and to settle opinions in philosophy or politics; but an *Arbiter elegantiarum*, a judge of propriety, was yet wanting, who should survey the track of daily conversation and free it from thorns and prickles, which tease the passer, though they do not wound him. (Greene, 649–50)

The *Tatler* and *Spectator* provided a standard of 'propriety and politeness' and exhibited the 'Characters and Manners of the Age'. They also dealt with 'literature and criticism . . . and taught, with great justness of argument and dignity of language, the most important duties and sublime truths' (Greene, 650–1).

Johnson's appraisal highlights the social and moral functions of these periodicals, in teaching manners as well as ethics, but he also stresses the importance of the language and style in which this content was conveyed. He sees Steele and Addison as innovative because they developed a polite vernacular tradition for an audience that was not necessarily part of the classically educated elite that formed the readership of *London* and *The Vanity of Human Wishes*.

Peter Hohendahl and Terry Eagleton have emphasized the importance of these early eighteenth-century periodicals in the construction of an 'English bourgeois public sphere'. They argue that this era saw the development of a range of social institutions, such as clubs and coffee houses, in which the wealthy commercial and professional classes, whom they label the 'bourgeoisie', could meet together and exchange ideas. The effect of these institutions was to encourage the emergence of a sense of collective identity, and a distinct social and political ideology.[2] As Johnson's words indicate, the early periodicals had played a crucial role in moulding this sense of identity, by articulating the views and shaping the taste of an educated class that was distinct from the aristocratic elite that had traditionally monopolized political power and shaped public opinion. Yet, while periodicals often attacked the morality of the aristocracy, they did not set themselves up in direct opposition to aristocratic values and interests. Eagleton has argued that their 'major impulse is one of class-consolidation, a codifying of the norms and regulating of the practices whereby the English bourgeoisie may negotiate an historic alliance with its social superiors'.[3] Literature and social institutions can be seen as a means of fostering a sense of shared values and common identity between the aristocratic elite and the educated professionals and gentry. Yet Johnson's early periodical writings at least cannot be comfortably accommodated within this concept of an inclusive, bourgeois, public sphere.

Johnson's style is rather different from the easy informality that characterized the *Spectator*, particularly in the early *Rambler* papers. Johnson initially saw his journalistic project not as a means of reaching out to a wide audience, but as a serious moral crusade. His religious purpose is indicated by the prayer that he composed at its commencement: 'Almighty God, the giver of all good things, without whose help all Labour is ineffectual, and without whose grace all wisdom is folly, grant, I beseech Thee, that in this mine undertaking thy Holy Spirit may not be witheld from me, but that I may promote thy glory, and the Salvation both of myself and others (*Works*, i. 43). Accordingly, the early papers deal with rather more elevated moral and literary subjects than were customary in previous periodicals. This is revealed in the table of contents that was added to the *Rambler* by Johnson's publishers when it came out in volume form. We are given meditations on subjects such as 'Retirement natural to a great mind. Its religious use' (7) and 'The thoughts to be brought under regulation; as they respect the past, present and future' (8). The tone is weighty, replete with gravitas and Johnsonian expressions, and seems designed to exclude certain kinds of reader rather than to mould a public consensus. Terry Eagleton refers to its 'considerably glummer tone than the earlier periodicals, its loss of a certain effect of spontaneous sociability' and suggests that it was not designed to be widely popular.[4]

The following meditation on the motivation behind the project epitomizes the style of many of the early numbers. Johnson wants to tell his readers that he cannot wait to get on with his project. He tells us that: 'Having accurately weighed the reasons for arrogance and submission, I find them so nearly equiponderant, that my impatience to try the event of my first performance will not suffer me to attend any longer the trepidations of the balance' (*Works*, iii. 7). In such passages the shadow of the lexicographer seems to fall over the genial persona of the essayist and the result is an oratorical grandeur that is in striking contrast to the conversational tone adopted by Addison's Mr Spectator. The structure of the arguments is similarly complex. Paul Korshin describes the method of a typical essay as 'sermonlike, beginning with a quotation from or an allusion to a well-known author, and following with homiletic exposition, development, and didactic conclusion'.[5] Walter Jackson Bate suggests that the 'heavy' style of the pieces resulted from 'the frequent use of . . . abstract nouns and general terms' which was a consequence of the 'constant centripetal pull toward maxim or aphorism'.[6] Johnson wanted to use his essays to set out moral precepts for the guidance of his readers. He wanted to tell them how to behave, instead of addressing matters of taste that could lead to the emergence of a shared sense of cultural and ethical identity.

In *Rambler* 10, however, the narrative voice is diversified by the inclusion of four 'billets' – short letters that were supposedly written to the Rambler, inquiring his opinion on topics relating more to manners and social conduct than to ethics and morality. There are reflections on card parties and an ironic encomium on the masquerade, in response to the enquiry of the correspondent Flirtilla. These billets were written by Johnson's friend Hester Mulso and include the wish that 'he would condescend to the weakness of minds softened by perpetual amusements, and now and then throw in, like his predecessor [the Spectator], some papers of a gay and humorous turn' (*Works*, iii. 52). I would argue that the subsequent papers show an inclination to respond to this request, as Johnson seeks to employ a narrative tone that, if not 'gay and humorous', is less uniformly weighty than in the early numbers. The diction is still essentially Johnsonian, but there is some diversification of the subject matter.

In Number 12 Johnson devotes an entire issue to a letter supposedly written by the daughter of a country gentleman, recounting her difficulties seeking a position as a servant in London. The story exposes the incivility and inhumanity of the elite towards their social inferiors and, since it is put into the mouth of a young, naive, and female character, it is told with relative clarity and simplicity. The epistolary technique proved effective and, in all, sixty-three of the 208 *Ramblers* were either partly or wholly written in the form of a fictitious letter to the editor, including some of the well-known numbers that have been most frequently anthologized. This was not an entirely new departure. Letters from correspondents had been a popular and significant component of both the *Tatler* and *Spectator*, but, while some of the letters to these early periodicals were probably written by real readers, Johnson's were all wholly fictitious.

The inclusion of the letters made it possible for Johnson to get away from the public and serious tone of the character of 'Mr Rambler' himself. In writing in the guise of various fictional correspondents, Johnson could explore different characters, and, to some extent, different voices. This is manifest, for example, in the story of Misella, the prostitute, which extended over numbers 170 and 171. Misella's reflections on her condition manifest both the persistence of Johnson's characteristic diction, and his movement into new areas of experience. She exclaims that she is:

> The drudge of extortion and the sport of drunkenness; sometimes the property of one man, and sometimes the common prey of accidental lewdness; at one time tricked up for sale by the mistress of a brothel, at another begging in the streets to be relieved from hunger by wickedness; without any hope in the day but of finding some whom folly or excess may expose to my allurements, and without any reflections at night but such as guilt and terror impress upon me.   (Greene, 256)

These lines reflect Johnson's fondness for big words and Latinate phrasing, and the long sentence, with its series of subordinate clauses, has the classically derived structure that has been identified as a defining feature of his writing.[7] Nonetheless, the effect is powerful, because these words come from a fictitious character who speaks from experience, and their impact is heightened by the preceding tragic and personal narrative. Instead of arguing on the basis of abstract precepts and moral truths, Johnson enforces his message through story. Instead of focusing on purely public and moral issues, he could exploit a vein of pathos and humanity that to some extent anticipated the development of the novel of sentiment.

The fictitious correspondents are frequently female, and the problems on which they write tend to be private and familial rather than public and political. Paul Korshin suggests that Johnson 'found the feminine persona a convenient way to represent the less public sphere that eighteenth-century women occupied' and notes the large number of essays that deal with the issue of marriage.[8] *Rambler* 35, for instance, explores the consequences of 'A Marriage of Prudence without Affection'.

Johnson is therefore using the form of the periodical essay to explore questions of marriage and sexuality that were becoming the subject matter of the emergent genre of the novel.

Within the confines of the *Rambler*, Johnson could put on female personae and to some extent female voices, and explore areas of feminine concern. Samuel Richardson had popularized the 'novel in letters', or epistolary narrative, with the publication of *Pamela* (1740) and *Clarissa* (1747–8), so that letters were becoming closely associated with fiction, and with the exploration of private and essentially female preoccupations. Yet, while his periodical increasingly exploited the techniques of the novel form, Johnson provides an account of the development of the genre in a famous essay in *Rambler* 4 that shows considerable uncertainty over the moral and social implications of fiction.

Johnson starts the essay by defining those 'works of fiction, with which the present generation seems more particularly delighted'. They are 'such as exhibit life in its true state, diversified only by accidents that daily happen in the world, and influenced by passions and qualities which are really to be found in conversing with mankind' (Greene, 175). These are contrasted with the earlier tradition of heroic romance, which is characterized as incredible and formulaic. Yet, although modern fiction is distinguished by its 'accurate observation of the living world', Johnson is anxious to make it clear that this 'is not the most important concern that an author of this sort ought to have before him' (Greene, 176):

> These books are written chiefly to the young, the ignorant, and the idle, to whom they serve as lectures of conduct, and introductions into life. They are the entertainments of minds unfurnished with ideas, and therefore easily susceptible of impressions; not fixed by principles, and therefore easily following the current of fancy; not informed by experience, and consequently open to every false suggestion and partial account.   (Greene, 176)

Although Johnson was to use the *Rambler* to develop fictional voices that could explore the issues of ordinary private life, he expresses in this early number a view of the readership of fiction that suggests that he sees it as clearly distinct from the audience of his own work. We, the readers of the *Rambler*, are being asked to observe the readers of fiction as a distinct and definable group, and as one that is peculiarly liable to misinterpret literary texts. As a result, Johnson cautions against the use of fiction to portray characters that, while resembling nature, are morally misleading. He urges that the world should not be 'promiscuously described', for:

> It is . . . not a sufficient vindication of a character, that it is drawn as it appears, for many characters ought never to be drawn; nor of a narrative, that the train of events is agreeable to observation and experience, for that observation which is called knowledge of the world, will be found much more frequently to make men cunning than good. (Greene, 177)

Instead of creating characters that are a mixture of good and bad qualities, authors should concentrate on figures that exhibit 'the most perfect idea of virtue'. This virtue should be 'not angelical, nor above probability . . . but the highest and purest that humanity can reach'. Likewise, 'vice . . . should always disgust; nor should the graces of gaiety, or the dignity of courage, be so united with it, as to reconcile it to the mind.' (Greene, 178)

These literary strictures have been interpreted as Johnson's contribution to the mid-eighteenth-century debate over the relative merits of the novelists Samuel Richardson and Henry Fielding. Fielding's *Tom Jones* contained a portrait of the kind of 'mixed character' that Johnson disavows. Tom Jones has moral failings, particularly in relation to the opposite sex, but these are combined with 'graces of gaiety' and 'the dignity of courage'. In contrast, Richardson's *Clarissa* presents, in its eponymous heroine, a portrait of virtue 'the highest and purest that humanity can reach' (Greene, 178).

Boswell's *Life* contains accounts of several conversations in which Johnson compared Fielding unfavourably to Richardson, but his belief in the immorality of Fielding's work is dependent on his characterization of the audience of fiction as incapable of moral discrimination. Fielding develops a fictional form that is inherently empiricist. His heroes have a natural predisposition towards virtue, but they learn how to behave correctly only through the experiences that are contained in the novel. After a chastening series of events, they learn the error of their ways, so that by the end of the novels they are models of moral probity. Moreover, the reader, having vicariously participated in the experiences of the characters, is expected also to have acquired knowledge and judgement and to be likewise morally improved. In contrast, Richardson's heroine is the epitome of virtue from the start of the book, and her ghastly experiences serve only to expose and prove her virtue.[9] Richardson's *Clarissa* was to be immensely influential in the development of the novel, popularizing the epistolary form and the importance of sentiment within fiction. Yet Fielding's emphasis on experience was perhaps a more lasting legacy, leading to the *Bildungsroman*, or apprenticeship novel, of the nineteenth century, which charted the development of a young mind towards maturity.[10] Johnson's *Rambler* 4 is an articulate rejection of the didactic potential of experience as a narrative device. This suggests that, despite the willingness to accept new methods of literary production and distribution that has been emphasized by Alvin Kernan, and despite his willingness to experiment with different narrative personae within the *Rambler*, Johnson retained a deep suspicion of the readership that lay beyond the narrow circle of the classically educated elite. He did not have sufficient faith in the discriminatory powers of this audience to desire the development of a consensual public sphere.

In *Rambler* 60, Johnson examines 'The dignity and usefulness of biography'. He argues that 'no species of writing seems more worthy of cultivation ... since none can be more delightful or more useful, none can more certainly enchain the heart by irresistible interest, or more widely diffuse instruction to every diversity of condition' (Greene, 204). He describes the process by which the narrative of an individual life can provide instruction:

> All joy or sorrow for the happiness or calamities of others is produced by an act of the imagination, that realises the event however fictitious, or approximates it however remote, by placing us, for a time, in the condition of him whose fortune we contemplate; so that we feel, while the deception lasts, whatever motions would be excited by the same good or evil happening to ourselves. (Greene, 204)

Such biographies are not to be confined to those figures of exemplary virtue and abhorrent vice that were recommended for inclusion in the novel. Johnson suggests 'that there has rarely passed a life of which a judicious and faithful narrative would not be useful' (Greene, 205) and he had himself written the biography of Richard Savage, a man who was, as Paul Korshin observes, 'plainly addicted to vice'.[11] The terms in which Johnson himself describes Savage in his *Life* can be taken as a definition of a 'mixed' character. He was 'a man equally distinguished by his virtues and vices, and at once remarkable for his weaknesses and abilities' (Greene, 160).

This raises the question of why Johnson represents the story of a real 'mixed' or faulty character as a source of moral enlightenment, while the story of a fictional one is presented in *Rambler* 4 as a potential threat to the ethical fabric of society. The distinction does not seem to derive from differences in the audience of the two forms, for, although the readership of fiction is represented as more or less exclusively comprised of 'the young, the ignorant and the idle', we are told that the lessons of biography can be applied 'to every diversity of condition'.

One explanation for this apparent contradiction could be related to the difference in the narrative style of the two forms. While the writer of biography can use the individual history to exemplify moral precepts and make explicit moral judgements, the narrator of fiction tended to have a much less overtly didactic role. This was particularly the case in works such as Fielding's *Tom Jones*, where the narrative voice was both source and subject of irony. Despite the construction of the figure of a narrator who was controlling and authoritative, it was incumbent on the reader to decipher the true message of the text.[12] The egalitarian nature of the relationship between narrator and reader is indicated in the opening chapter of the final book of *Tom Jones*, in which both reader and narrator are exhorted to 'behave to one another like fellow-travellers in a stage-coach, who have passed several days in the company of each other; and who, notwithstanding any bickerings or little animosities which may have occurred on the road, generally make all up at last, and mount, for the last time, into their vehicle with chearfulness and good-humour'.[13]

In contrast, the narrator of Johnson's *Account of the Life of Mr Richard Savage* uses the conclusion of the narrative to draw out its moral implications for the guidance and edification of the reader. The character of Savage is evaluated, so that the virtues and vices are clearly distinguished and separated, and the deleterious impact of the latter on the former is demonstrated. The overall effect is of a judge's summing-up. We are told that:

> His temper was in consequence of the dominion of his passions uncertain and capricious; he was easily engaged, and easily disgusted; but he is accused of retaining his hatred more tenaciously than his benevolence.
>
> He was compassionate both by nature and principle and always ready to perform offices of humanity, but when he was provoked, and very small offences were sufficient to provoke him, he would prosecute his revenge with the utmost acrimony till his passion had subsided.   (Greene, 162)

His works are evaluated in similarly even-handed terms, his versification being 'sonorous and majestic' but also 'sluggish and encumbered'; his style harsh yet dignified; his sentiments sublime yet uniform (Green, 163). Johnson concludes by stressing the moral utility of the narrative, both to those who feel that they have suffered in the same way as Savage, and to those who feel that they are above such suffering. The former 'shall be enabled to fortify their patience by reflecting that they feel only those afflictions from which the abilities of Savage did not exempt him', while the latter 'shall be reminded that nothing will supply the want of prudence, and that negligence and irregularity long continued will make knowledge useless, wit ridiculous, and genius contemptible' (Greene, 164). These words are ironically similar to those of Mr Allworthy at the end of Fielding's *Tom Jones*, when he declares that:

> Prudence is indeed the duty which we owe to ourselves; and if we will be so much our own enemies as to neglect it, we are not to wonder if the world is deficient in discharging their duty to us; for when a man lays the foundation of his own ruin, others will, I am afraid, be too apt to build upon it.[14]

But, whereas Allworthy's words represent one perspective, which the events of the narrative appear to subvert, the words of Johnson's narrator have the force of an indisputable moral truth.

Johnson's suspicion of the moral impact of fiction, despite his own fondness for reading romances (*Life*, 36), may derive from an uncertainty over the readerly autonomy that was implicit in the form. The young and ignorant readership that Johnson associated with the genre was identified as inherently incapable of the exercise of moral discrimination that such narratives required. Although, therefore, Johnson may be characterized as a forward-looking writer, who embraced new markets and new technology, an examination of the *Rambler* suggests that this was only half the story. There is also evidence of more reactionary attitudes towards literature and language.

Rambler 168, which is devoted to an exploration of the language of Shakespeare, exposes Johnson's desire to maintain standards of literary decorum. This essay has been taken by some critics to epitomize the limitations of the eighteenth-century neoclassical approach to literature, and Johnson has been mocked for his attack on Shakespeare's down-to-earth vocabulary. The Rambler argues that all readers are inevitably alienated when an author incorporates 'low terms', claiming that truth 'loses much of her power over the soul when she appears disgraced by a dress uncouth or ill-adjusted'. To exemplify this argument, Johnson cites the speech of Lady Macbeth that heralds the murder of the King:

> Come, thick night!
> And pall thee in the dunnest smoke of hell,
> That my keen knife see not the wound it makes;
> Nor heav'n peep through the blanket of the dark,
> To cry, hold, hold!
>
> (*Macbeth*, I. v. 48–52)

Johnson argues that any reader would find the force of this passage weakened by the use of 'dun' – 'an epithet now seldom heard but in the stable'; 'knife' – a word that was connected with 'sordid offices'; and 'blanket' – which apparently Johnson could not hear without risibility.

While Johnson had recognized, earlier in the article, that there is no general agreement over what constitutes 'low' language, he nonetheless suggests that these words will inevitably displease, because of their association with humble objects and mean circumstances. The *Rambler* article therefore hints at a notion of linguistic propriety that seems to derive from neoclassical concepts of what is appropriate or fitting within literature. As such, it seems at odds with the emphasis on inclusive language and cultural consensus that formed the essence of the earlier tradition of periodical writing. It also suggests a more rigid adherence to neoclassical tenets than was later to be found in the preface to Johnson's edition of Shakespeare's plays. Between the *Rambler* essay of 26 October 1751 and the publication of the preface in 1765 there may have been some moderation of Johnson's critical philosophy and a recognition that the conventions derived from analysis of the Greek and Latin classics may not invariably represent appropriate standards for the evaluation of works for the modern stage.

The *Rambler* represents an excursion into a form that, in its origins, was popular, vernacular, and market oriented, but the resultant papers are far from populist. J. C. D. Clark has indicated the numerous references to Renaissance humanists like Bellarmine, Camerarius, Cardano, Castiglione, Cornaro, Cujacius, Descartes, Erasmus, Fabricius, Gassendi, Lipsius, Politian, Pontanus, Sannazaro, the Scaligers, and Thuanus.[15] Bate and Strauss have analysed the 669 quotations and literary allusions in the *Rambler* and discovered that 60 per cent are from Greek and classical Latin authors. Of the 251 quotations from, and references to, works written since the beginning of the Renaissance, only thirty-seven are to eighteenth-century writers.[16] Johnson engages with the marketplace to the extent that he adopts the form that had been so successfully exploited by Steele and Addison, but he uses it to address a readership with whom these references will resonate.

Johnson's enthusiasm for developments in print technology was combined with suspicion of the interpretative capacity of the expanding reading public. While he used the periodical form to experiment with female personae and the exploration of private rather than public experience, these fictional excursions were circumscribed by the *Rambler* format. The voices of the correspondents, describing significant events in their lives, were balanced by the moral precepts and didactic utterances of Mr Rambler himself, and his narrative was clearly devised to appeal to a limited readership. The *Rambler* therefore embodies the literary potential of personal experience, but also the moral anxieties that surrounded the development of the fictional form. It represents Johnson's desire to address a wider readership, but also his perception of the moral responsibilities involved in doing so.

Later in his life, from 15 April 1758 to 5 April 1760, Johnson produced another series of weekly essays, under the title of the *Idler*, as part of a new weekly newspaper, the *Universal Chronicle*. Perhaps as a response to the criticisms of the *Rambler*, or in recognition of the widening audience for periodical literature, the *Idler* essays are shorter, and lighter in tone, than the earlier pieces. They have fewer classical references, less complex sentence structure, and not as many polysyllabic words. J. C. D. Clark suggests that in the *Idler* Johnson 'consciously sought an easy vernacular style', which has been seen as 'a deliberate attempt to match the relaxed and informal idiom of Addison and Steele'.[17] Yet this did not mean that the papers were necessarily light or trivial in content. Composed during the Seven Years War, which saw massive slaughter in Europe, Johnson used papers such as Number 22, 'The Vulture's View of Man', and Number 81, 'European Oppression in America', to provide a biting and satirical indictment of the war and of government policy. DeMaria suggests that this political vituperation was made possible by the character of Mr Idler, which 'allows Johnson to address contemporary events more directly than he could as the philosophical Mr Rambler' (DeMaria, 197). While 'The Rambler is a monitor set above his readers and largely inaccessible to them . . . the Idler seems intellectually and ethically within reach' (DeMaria, 196).

Yet this does not mean that the *Idler* embraces a different or broader readership from that addressed in the *Rambler*. The maintenance of the earlier elitism is indicated in the second paper, which discusses the current vogue for literary composition amongst all sections of society. In describing how 'the cook warbles her lyricks in the kitchen, and the thrasher vociferates his heroicks in the barn . . . our traders deal out knowledge in bulky volumes, and our girls forsake their samplers to teach kingdoms wisdom' (*Works*, ii. 7), the Idler is clearly identifying the creativity of those outside the educated elite as unnatural, undesirable, and comical. A group that runs from domestic servants and agricultural labourers to tradesmen and young girls are clearly identified as 'other', subject to the satire of the Idler and his like-minded readers.

In appealing for contributions to his periodical, Mr Idler declares that he will solicit only from those 'who have already devoted themselves to literature, or, without any determinate attention, wander at large through the expanse of life' (*Works*, ii. 7). This represents people who share the idleness characteristic of the narrator, but such a denomination has social as well as moral or physiological connotations. Johnson does not seek contributions from those whose energies and horizons are tied to a particular calling so that they are not able to 'wander at large'. His ideal contributor may be naturally indolent, but he also has to be in a position to afford to be so. The *Idler* therefore adopts an easier, more conversational tone than the more austere *Rambler*, but this ease is connected with an idleness that is associated with the social status of the gentleman.

3

The *Dictionary*

Johnson's work on the *Rambler* and the *Idler* gave him a little light relief from his primary occupation in the period from 1746 to 1755 – the composition of his monumental *Dictionary*. This work finally established his position as a cultural giant in the eighteenth century and earned him his honorary doctorate and his nickname of Dictionary Johnson (*Life*, 272).

Although often proclaimed as the first work of its kind in England, this was by no means the case. Following the publication of Robert Cawdrey's *A Table Alphabeticall* in 1604, numerous books were published through the seventeenth century that provided lists of words and their definitions. These 'hard word books' focused on academic, technical, or unusual words, but in 1721 Nathan Bailey published *An Universall Etymological Dictionary*, which provided explanations of common as well as hard words. Yet there was still a feeling that Britain required a substantial and authoritative etymological study that could rival the dictionaries produced in Italy and France and establish the English language as a serious and scholarly tongue. J. C. D. Clark has argued that the *Dictionary* can be seen as a response to Johnson's recognition of the increasing irrelevance of the classics within the contemporary literary and political establishment. It was in part 'intended to be the foundation stone of a newly-strengthened vernacular culture, to replace the old: English was now to be raised to the dignity of Latin and Greek as a medium for cultural expression'.[1] A succession of writers, including Dryden, Defoe, Pope, and Swift, had argued the need for such a work and it can be seen as part of the interest in taxonomy, classification, and codifying that produced a range or works, such as the French

39

Encyclopédie, and the system of biological classification of the Swedish naturalist Carl Linnaeus. Michel Foucault has identified this preoccupation with tabulating and systematizing knowledge as a defining characteristic of the eighteenth century.

Alvin Kernan has stressed the importance of the *Dictionary* as 'the essential book of print'. It confirmed the importance of the print medium as a mechanism for the control of language and was thus 'a revelation of the metaphysics of print, its ability to abstract, order and idealize language'.[2] The *Dictionary* has, therefore, been taken as a monument to the commercial and entrepreneurial nature of culture within Britain, and as a sign of Johnson's immersion in this culture.

Johnson's book was significantly different from the dictionaries produced on the continent in the eighteenth century. Both the Italian *Vocabulario* (1623) and the French *Dictionnaire* (1694) were produced by groups of academics, working within learned institutions, with the aim of stabilizing their national language. Johnson's *Dictionary*, on the other hand, was the work of a single scholar, with half a dozen assistants, employed by a group of booksellers whose aim was to make a profit. The significance of this distinction has been stressed by recent critics and was emphasized by Johnson himself. Allen Reddick begins his detailed study of *The Making of Johnson's Dictionary 1746–1773* with Boswell's account of the conversation between Dr Adams and Johnson in which the former expressed a doubt that Johnson could complete the dictionary in three years, since 'the French Academy, which consists of forty members, took forty years to compile their Dictionary'. The reply came back: 'Sir, thus it is. This is the proportion. Let me see; forty times forty is sixteen hundred. As three to sixteen hundred, so is the proportion of an Englishman to a Frenchman' (*Life*, 135).[3] In fact, the *Dictionary* took almost ten years to complete, so the proportion was ten to sixteen hundred.

Despite Johnson's nationalistic bravado, the *Dictionary* was not composed without tremendous struggles, against personal tragedy and constitutional melancholy, but also against the intractability of language and its inherent resistance to the processes of abstracting, ordering, and idealizing. In the course of compiling the work, Johnson's ideas about the nature of language, as well as his personal circumstances, underwent significant changes.

Johnson began work on the *Dictionary* in early 1746 at the instigation of Robert Dodsley. He produced a 'short scheme' of the work, which was used to attract booksellers and printers to support the project. In June 1746 Johnson signed a contract with a group of London booksellers, who agreed to share the costs of production, and to pay Johnson £1,575 (*Life*, 132).[4] He in turn agreed to produce the book within three years. Although much of the publishers' advance was swallowed up in unavoidable expenses, such as the purchase of paper and the wages of the assistants, this money probably brought a long-awaited period of financial security to the Johnson household. Instead of a footloose existence, moving between temporary lodgings, occasionally dodging arrest and depending on pecuniary assistance from more affluent friends, Johnson was able to rent a substantial house at 17 Gough Square. He could employ servants and start living in a style that was appropriate to a gentleman of letters.

In early August 1747 Johnson published his *Plan of an English Dictionary*. This work can in one sense be taken to typify the *Dictionary* as a whole, in that it is written as part advertisement and part linguistic manifesto and thus embodies the combination of economic and scholarly motives by which Johnson was activated. It outlines the system by which he intends to arrange and categorise the various meanings and usages within the dictionary, and it details his aspirations for the project. It also concludes with a fulsome dedication to Philip Dormer Stanhope, 4th Earl of Chesterfield, whom Dodsley had persuaded Johnson to accept as patron. 'Whatever be the event of my endeavours', Johnson declares:

> I shall not easily regret an attempt which has procured me the honour of appearing thus publickly,
> *My Lord*,
> *Your Lordship's*
> *Most Obedient and*
> *Most Humble Servant*,
> SAM. JOHNSON[5]

In the following years Johnson's initial aims and aspirations were put to the test as he continued to work on the *Dictionary* and increasingly recognized the enormity of the task that he had undertaken. Some critics have suggested that these years saw a gradual alteration in Johnson's thinking about language, as he struggled with the difficulties of the project. At the same time there was a dramatic change in his attitude to Chesterfield and the institution of aristocratic patronage. The history of Johnson's relationship with Chesterfield has been taken as a symbol of wider developments in publishing in the eighteenth century, as patronage became redundant within an increasingly commercial industry.

The story has been often told. In response to the *Plan*, Chesterfield made Johnson a gift of ten pounds but then took no interest in the project for the next seven years, while Johnson struggled and laboured and despaired. Then, in 1754, as the *Dictionary* neared completion, Chesterfield came onto the scene again, apparently ready to resume the role of the patron of scholarship and gain his share of the credit. He wrote two articles, which appeared in Dodsley's journal, *The World*, on 28 November and 5 December 1754, praising Johnson and celebrating the *Dictionary*, but in a tone of light-hearted aristocratic flippancy. He recommended all those who could afford it to go out and buy the book and gave his own view of the need for the work and its social function. He observes that 'our language is at present in a state of anarchy' and that 'Good order and authority are now necessary'. Thus:

> We must have recourse to the Old Roman expedient in times of confusion, and chuse a dictator. Upon this principle, I give my vote for Mr Johnson to fill that great and arduous post. And I hereby declare that I make a total surrender of all my rights and privileges in the English language, as a free-born British subject, to the said Mr Johnson, during the term of his dictatorship. Nay more; I will not only obey him, like an old Roman, as my dictator, but like a modern Roman, I will implicitly believe in him as my pope, and hold him to be infallible while in the chair; but no longer.[6]

Chesterfield's words equate linguistic and political absolutism, but they also suggest that Johnson's work, far from being a permanent monument to scholarship and a lasting contribution to knowledge, will be only transitory in its effect and as ephemeral as a Pope.

Johnson's response took the form of a letter to Chesterfield, dated February 1755. This was a semi-public document, which both the writer and recipient circulated amongst their friends, and the latter displayed on his desk for the edification of visitors. The letter reveals Johnson's deep resentment at what he perceived to be Chesterfield's neglect over the arduous years of composition, followed by his attempt to jump on the bandwagon once all the work was done. He points out that for seven years he has been pushing on his work 'through difficulties, of which it is useless to complain'. He has 'brought it at last, to the verge of publication, without one act of assistance, one word of encouragement, or one smile of favour' (Greene, 782–3).[7] During the writing of the *Dictionary*, Johnson's wife, Tetty, had died, he had suffered great poverty, frustration, and isolation, but had gradually become established as a fairly well-known literary figure. As he tells Chesterfield: 'The notice which you have been pleased to take of my labours, had it been early, had been kind; but it has been delayed till I am indifferent and cannot enjoy it; till I am solitary, and cannot impart it; till I am known, and do not want it.'[8] The sense of personal injury is palpable, but Johnson's letter is not so much a manifestation of wounded pride and individual pique, as an attack on the relationship between patron and author that had for many years been central to literary production. Johnson represents his treatment by Chesterfield as typical of the exploitation inherent within this relationship. With heavy irony he comments 'Such treatment I did not expect, for I never had a patron before' and asks 'Is not a patron, my Lord, one who looks with unconcern on a man struggling for life in the water and when he has reached ground encumbers him with help?'

Johnson's letter has been celebrated as a crucial moment in literary history, signalling the end of the system of literary patronage and the establishment of a commercial, market-based system. For Kernan it is 'the Magna Carta of the modern author'.[9] Of course, such claims can be exaggerated. The patronage system had been in decline for many years, and was to stagger on for some time longer. Nonetheless, the letter indicates a significant shift in the concept of the author, particularly when compared to the fawning tone of the 1747

Plan, with its appeals to 'my Lord ... whose authority in our language is so generally acknowledged'. By 1755, Johnson was 'unwilling that the Publick should consider me as owing that to a Patron which Providence has enabled me to do for myself'. It is not merely that the new print economy made book production possible without aristocratic assistance. The letter indicates that, by the time the *Dictionary* was published, Johnson felt that he had established himself and his work sufficiently for them to be judged on their own merits. As such, it indicates the growing importance of the author as a figure who could endow a text with authority, without requiring the endorsement of a patron. Weinbrot and Reddick have argued that this reflects the change in Johnson's status that took place in the period from 1746 to 1755, but it may also indicate the growing social importance of the man of letters within eighteenth-century society.[10]

The Johnson/Chesterfield debacle has a further significance in that it highlights the extent to which Johnson's concept of language and of the function of the dictionary had changed in the course of its composition. Chesterfield's reference to Johnson as a 'dictator', whose role was to impose order on a disordered language, bears no relation to Johnson's practice, but it is closer to the idea of the dictionary outlined in the *Plan* than to that developed in the preface to the first edition.

The preface is an eloquent narrative of Johnson's personal struggle to construct the *Dictionary* and his gradual redefinition of his aims. He describes the initial impetus behind the project, which is ascribed to his belief that, while English literature was widely cultivated, the language had fallen into neglect. Like an unpruned plant, it had been 'suffered to spread, under the direction of chance, into wild exuberance' (Greene, 307). The dictionary compiler is represented as one whose task is to sort out the mess and make order out of this wild confusion. Yet the language in which Johnson describes his first idea of the role of the lexicographer contains echoes of the authoritarian terminology of Chesterfield's facetious notion of the linguistic dictator: 'When I took the first survey of my undertaking, I found our speech copious without order, and energetic without rules: wherever I turned my view, there was perplexity to be disentangled, and confusion to be regulated; choice was to be made out of boundless variety, without any established principle of selection' (Greene, 307). While slightly daunted by the task, Johnson presents himself as haunted by a desire to restrain linguistic change. His assertions that language is inherently mutable are interspersed by rather wistful yearnings that it could be otherwise:

> I am not yet so lost in lexicography as to forget that *words are the daughters of earth, and that things are the sons of heaven*. Language is only the instrument of science, and words are but the signs of ideas: I wish, however, that the instrument might be less apt to decay, and that signs might be permanent, like the things which they denote. (Greene, 310)

The process of compiling the *Dictionary* entailed a retreat from the desire, expressed in the *Plan*, to fix language, towards a more modest aspiration to restrain the rate of change (Greene, 324). In part this retreat was an inevitable consequence of Johnson's method of compilation.

Robert DeMaria indicates the significance of Johnson's decision to illustrate the meaning of words by examples from literature rather than with illustrations specially composed for the purpose. The consequence was that, unlike the French *Dictionnaire*, words were explained through actual usage rather than ideal usage. For instance, the word 'Fairy', in its adjectival form, is explained as:

> 1. Given by fairies.
>   Be secret and discrete; these *fairy* favours
> Are lost when not conceal'd. *Dryd. Spanish Friar.*
>   Such borrowed wealth, like *fairy* money, though it were gold in the hand from which he received it, will be but leaves and dust when it comes to use. *Locke.*
> 2. Belonging to fairies.
>   This is the *fairy* land: oh, spight of spights,
> We talk with goblins, owls, and elvish sprights. *Shakespeare.*

After the basic definition, the meaning is illustrated through examples of how the word has been used, by Dryden, Locke, and Shakespeare, rather than through a hypothetical instance. This reflects Johnson's belief in the importance of print rather than oral culture, but it can also be read as a recognition that language derives its meaning from the way that it is used and thus can never be restrained or controlled. As DeMaria points out, 'theoretically, according to such an ideal, every usage of a word counts as much as any other'.[11] Instead of having an ideal meaning, or group of meanings, from which individual usage might diverge, there could in theory be as many shades of meaning as there are uses of the word. So, instead of being a dictator of meaning, who fixed the language and settled the spelling, pronunciation, and definition of words, the dictionary compiler was an archivist, whose task was to catalogue the uses that he found and reflect rather than shape the language of the world.

Alvin Kernan has identified considerable ideological significance in Johnson's evolving notion of language. He argues that:

> We can see from the 1755 'Preface' that Johnson discovered some things about 'a living speech' that he did not know when he wrote the 1747 *Plan*, and these discoveries inevitably changed his sense of the relationship of the language to the highest social class. A language, he found, has a democratic basis, existing finally only in the mouths and hands of the many.[12]

This seems to overstate the case, for, while the preface moves away from the implicit authoritarianism of the *Plan*, it can also be read as an emphatic rejection of any notion that language should have a 'democratic basis', or that the role of the lexicographer is to enshrine the words of the 'many'. Johnson's growing realization that he would not be able to incorporate *all* words within his book, and his explanation of the kind of words he would represent, constitutes another facet of the narrative of resignation of the preface.

Johnson recounts how, at the start of the project, he aspired to provide total coverage, including all the words from all aspects of life and areas of knowledge. He provides a vivid account of the enthusiasm and ambition with which he embarked upon this project:

> I resolved to leave neither words nor things unexamined, and pleased myself with a prospect of the hours which I should revel away in feasts of literature, the obscure recesses of northern learning which I should enter and ransack, the treasures with which I expected every search into those neglected mines to

reward my labour, and the triumph with which I should display my acquisitions to mankind. (Greene, 321)

In addition he would:

> Pierce deep into every science ... inquire the nature of every substance of which I inserted the name ... limit every idea by a definition strictly logical and exhibit every production of art or nature in an accurate description, that my book might be in place of all other dictionaries whether appellative or technical. (Greene, 321–2)

This sounds more like an encyclopaedia than a dictionary, and Johnson's recognition of the impossibility of this plan is encapsulated in his famous remark that 'these were the dreams of a poet doomed at last to wake a lexicographer' (Greene, 322). It is too late for Johnson to learn all the arts and all the sciences, to read all books (including those from the north of Britain), and find out about all objects. He cannot include *all* language, so this raises the question of which language, or rather, whose language, will be included in the *Dictionary*.

The preface gives a clear indication of whose language will not be included. The *Dictionary* will not contain the 'many terms of art and manufacture' on the grounds that Johnson 'could not visit caverns to learn the miner's language, nor take a voyage to perfect [his] skill in the dialect of navigation, nor visit the warehouses of merchants, and shops of artificers, to gain the names of commodities, utensils, tools, and operations of which no mention is found in books' (Greene, 323). He cannot be expected to investigate the realms of trade and commerce to become acquainted with the language of the working people. To do so would have involved 'contesting with the sullenness of one, and the roughness of another'. But this omission is not represented as regrettable. The exclusion is justified on the grounds that the diction of the 'laborious and mercantile part of the people' is 'in great measure casual and mutable'. The terminologies of trade and manufacture change as the techniques and processes develop and alter. But there is also a suggestion that the laborious and mercantile classes are themselves 'casual' and unlikely to make great efforts to maintain the purity and stability of their own particular language. As a result, it 'cannot be regarded as any part of the durable materials of a language, and therefore must be suffered to perish with other things unworthy of preservation' (Greene, 323).

The corruption of language is identified as a consequence of commerce, which brings new goods and processes and contact with foreigners. But it is also caused by changes in the intellectual climate, with the expansion of knowledge and the cultivation of science and literature (Greene, 325). Johnson therefore finds himself in the position of having to select a particular kind of language, from a range of variant and shifting forms and dialects. The language that he ultimately chooses to include in the *Dictionary* is, simply, 'what favourable accident or easy inquiry brought within my reach' (Greene, 323). It is the language that Johnson came across in his normal life, in the rather restricted world of literary London. More particularly, it is the language of the books that Johnson read, with examples drawn from the great writers of the late sixteenth to the eighteenth century, culled from '*the wells of English undefiled*' (Greene, 319).[13] Far from being the language of the many, this represents the language of a very limited sector of society, the polite, educated elite. It is the language of hands and not of mouths. John Barrell suggests that this rejection of the language of the people has political implications:

> The stability of the language of the *polite*, and the stability of their constitution, are alike threatened by the mutability of the people, who properly considered, have no interest in either matter. They are no part of the true language community, which is now a closed circle of the polite whose language is now presented as durable and permanent; and they form no part of the political community.[14]

Yet, while Johnson clearly yearns for a language that is durable and permanent, and a constitution that is likewise, the preface is resonant with the realization that the one is as chimerical as the other:

> When we see men grow old and die at a certain time one after another, from century to century, we laugh at the elixir that promises to prolong life to a thousand years; and with equal justice may the lexicographer be derided who being able to produce no

example of a nation that has preserved their words and phrases from mutability shall imagine that his dictionary can embalm his language, and secure it from corruption and decay. (Greene, 324)

Preservation is here metaphorically equated with death and mummification – a superstitious desire to evade the signs of decay rather than a true extension of life. Given that language is seen as inherently liable to change, it becomes imperative that the definition of the national tongue is restricted to those who are seen as best able to resist the forces of corruption.

Robert DeMaria has argued that the prose writers chosen to appear in the *Dictionary*, such as Bacon, Hooker, Clarendon, Tillotson, Dryden, Temple, Locke, Sprat, Atterbury, Addison, and Swift, were 'a fairly predictable list of writers acknowledged for their excellence as stylists and, by and large, for their widely accepted, mainstream political and religious views'.[15] Johnson felt a moral responsibility towards his readers, whom he conceptualized as young and impressionable. He was also anxious to maximize sales and therefore tended to select quotations that were either uncontentious in themselves, or rendered uncontentious by being removed from their original context. Nonetheless, some of the early critics saw the book as a compilation of High Church, Tory sentiments, written to further a particular political cause. Reddick's extensive research into the way Johnson revised the *Dictionary* through its various editions charts an increasing reliance on conservative religious writers as the source of illustrative examples, noting 'the remarkable infusion of theological passages . . . into the revised work'.[16] Yet Reddick argues that any attempt to make the book into a political or religious polemic was 'for the most part diffused and defeated by the text itself'.[17] The book was too diverse, and language too resistant and multivocal, for Johnson to be able to present a clear ethic or ideology. As DeMaria argues, 'the *Dictionary* has the effect of reconciling political opponents and reducing extremist views to a gathering mainstream of belief'.[18]

Johnson initially aspired to form the *Dictionary* as a general work of reference in which every quotation would be 'useful to some other end than the illustration of a word' (Greene, 318), but this was another instance in which the ultimate achievement departed from the initial aims. He recognizes in the preface that all he can do is include some passages which will serve as flowers amid the 'dusty deserts of barren philology' (Greene, 318). But what the *Dictionary* does enshrine is an ideology of language, and one that is clearly distinct from that of Chesterfield.

Johnson's retreat from his initial aspiration to fix and control language is accompanied by a retreat from the desire for total coverage as well as from the hope that the book would have a wider moral role. While authority is located in usage, authoritative use is identified with only a limited sector of society and a limited group of writers. The lexicographer is constructed not so much as an arbiter of language as an arbiter of literature, determining which texts deserve to be included in the exemplary band. In this respect, Johnson's dictionary work can be seen as part of his wider project of establishing a canon of English literature but also embodies his ambivalent attitude to language. He was simultaneously anxious to extend access to the print medium, and yet restrict control over words that were seen as alarmingly unstable. As Allen Reddick argues: 'Johnson had no illusions about the *Dictionary* as a permanent fixed monument any more than he considered the language itself to be complete and unchanging; instead he thought of his *Dictionary* as organic and growing, striving for fullness and completion yet doomed to failure.'[19]

Yet the construction of the *Dictionary*, with its select band of exemplary writers, contributed to the creation of a notion of English, as opposed to Latin or Greek, classics. Sidney, Shakespeare, Dryden, Addison, and Pope were seen as part of an English tradition of literary excellence, and one within which Johnson himself could perhaps ultimately be located.

4

Rasselas

Johnson's next major work to be published after the *Dictionary* and the *Idler* essays was a philosophical tale, *The History of Rasselas, Prince of Abyssinia*, described by William Hazlitt as 'the most melancholy and debilitating moral speculation that ever was put forth'.[1] Boswell recounts that it was written in the evenings of a single week following the death of Johnson's mother in 1759, to raise money to pay for her funeral and settle her debts (*Life*, 240–1). Boswell's account may or may not be true – other biographers give slightly different versions of the story – but it serves to foster the image of *Rasselas* as a piece of occasional writing, a *jeu d'esprit*, rather than a weighty philosophical work.[2] It would appear from the various stories that Johnson was anxious to emphasize that the genre of narrative fiction did not require study or application from a mind such as his. *Rasselas* was merely the work of a few odd hours, so Johnson could not be considered as a writer of novels.

Moreover, while Boswell presented this account of the casual nature of the work's composition, he also highlighted its philosophical profundity, in terms that indicated that it was not to be considered as just a prose romance. He tells us:

> The fund of thinking which this work contains is such, that almost every sentence of it may furnish a subject of long meditation. I am not satisfied if a year passes without my having read it through; and at every perusal, my admiration of the mind which produced it is so highly raised, that I can scarcely believe that I had the honour of enjoying the intimacy of such a man. (*Life*, 242)

Rasselas is a meditative and intellectually inspiring work. Yet, despite the attempts of both Boswell and Johnson to distinguish it from the emergent genre of the novel, or prose romance, its economic success was probably in part a consequence of the enthusiasm for 'Oriental Tales' in the early eighteenth century. These had become very popular with the publication of works such as Antoine Galland's French translation of the *Arabian Nights – Les Mille et une nuits* from 1704 to 1717, and the translation by Ambrose Philips and others of the *Persian Tales* from French to English. There were *Turkish Tales*, *Chinese Tales*, and *Mogul Tales*, although, as Carey McIntosh remarks, 'most of the stories ... were no more oriental than Louis XIV's wig'.[3] They used exotic locations and an action-packed, fairy-tale format to create exciting, escapist entertainment. But the interest in the Orient also generated more intellectual works that explored moral and philosophical themes. Joseph Addison contributed oriental tales to the *Spectator*,[4] and Johnson's *Rambler* included four fables with Asiatic settings,[5] as well as 'The History of ten days of Seged, Emperor of Ethiopia'. This extended over two *Rambler* numbers and explored the theme of the quest for happiness.[6] The *Idler* likewise contained two Eastern tales.[7] These fables exploited the enormous interest in the foreign and exotic[8] that was manifested in the massive popularity of books of travels, both real and imaginary.[9] But, in many of these works, the anthropological interest in different people and places was combined with an allegorical exploitation of the foreign, for the customs and characteristics of another country could be used to explore the moral, philosophical, and ideological uncertainties of one's own. A version of this technique was exploited by Jonathan Swift in *Gulliver's Travels*, which used the fictional lands of Lilliput, Brobdingnag, Laputa, and Houyhnhnmland as satirical embodiments of aspects of the contemporary political and social system.

Johnson's first published work had been a translation, from French to English, of Father Lobo's *Voyage to Abyssinia* (1735), and elements of this and other travel works are used as a source for some of the details in *Rasselas*. But the tale is not primarily intended as an accurate account of life in Abyssinia. Like the *Rambler* pieces, it is essentially a moral work, using an exotic setting to explore philosophical questions about the nature of human existence. It therefore combines aspects of an escapist, popular, romance genre with moral and religious reflections addressed to a much more limited elite audience that would have seen itself as clearly distinct from the readership of the oriental prose romance.

The story tells of Prince Rasselas and his sister, Nekayah, who, in accordance with the custom of their country, are kept in a beautiful palace in a spacious valley, surrounded on all sides by mountains. 'Happy Valley' is described as a post-lapsarian Garden of Eden, in which 'all the diversities of the world were brought together, the blessings of nature were collected, and its evils extracted and excluded'.[10] Kids bound, monkeys frolic, and elephants repose. As well as these joys of nature, the valley is blessed with the highest achievements of human art. The best musicians, dancers and artificers are always on hand to divert the inhabitants so that 'revelry and merriment was the business of every hour from the dawn of morning to the close of even' (ch. 2, p. 337).

Yet even while the life of the inhabitants of the Happy Valley is portrayed as one long series of pleasures, we, the readers, are given a more sinister view of the Palace in which they live. We are told that it 'was built as if suspicion herself had dictated the plan'. It is a monument to secrecy and deception: 'To every room there was an open and secret passage, every square had a communication with the rest, either from the upper stories by private galleries, or by subterranean passages from the lower apartments' (ch. 1, p. 336). The source of the suspicion is avarice, for we are informed, in a passage that is reminiscent of the tradition of political satire as much as moral philosophy, that:

> Many of the columns had unsuspected cavities, in which a long race of monarchs had reposited their treasures. They then closed up the opening with marble, which was never to be removed but in the utmost exigencies of the kingdom; and recorded their accumulations in a book which was itself concealed in a tower not entered but by the emperor attended by the prince who stood next in succession. (ch. 1, pp. 336–7)

Behind the Edenic façade of an harmonious natural world is the all-too-human reality of a miserly materialism, so that even within the opening chapter the evocation of the ideal is undermined, foreshadowing the subsequent development of the plot.

For the inhabitants of the valley, however, there is no apparent alloy. The princes and princesses 'lived only to know the soft vicissitudes of pleasure and repose, attended by all that were skilful to delight, and gratified with whatever the senses can enjoy' (ch. 2, p. 337). Yet, despite this incessant entertainment, Rasselas is unhappy in the Happy Valley. He finds that 'pleasure has ceased to please' (ch. 3, p. 339) and he becomes obsessed with a desire to escape. This discontent can be taken to symbolize the restlessness and disappointment that Johnson portrays as inherent features of the human lot. True happiness is represented as alien to man's nature. Mankind will always be striving for something beyond what they already have, and the ultimate suffering derives from a situation in which there is nothing for which we can strive. This condition is conveyed in chapter three, 'The Wants of Him that Wants Nothing', a title that plays with the fact that, although in Johnson's day 'want' conventionally meant 'lack', it was also beginning to acquire its modern sense of 'desire'.

The narrative does not invariably endorse Rasselas's discontent, however. While it is clear that we are expected to sympathize with the prince, and see him as a symbol of the human condition, his melancholy is also the subject of some satire. There is a degree of irony in the account of how Rasselas 'passed four months in resolving to lose no more time in idle resolves, and was awakened to more vigorous exertion by hearing a maid who had broken a porcelain cup remark that what cannot be repaired is not to be regretted' (ch. 4, p. 342). After having resolved not to resolve, Rasselas is brought to his senses by the simple folk wisdom of the maid, the consequence of which is that he 'for a few hours, regretted his regret' (ch. 4, p. 342). The bantering tone of these lines suggests that, while *Rasselas* explores the misery that is seen to be an inevitable aspect of the human condition, and poses the question 'What is happiness?', it simultaneously satirizes such explorations and questionings. The words of the maid can be taken as a riposte to Johnson's text as a whole.

After a number of unsuccessful efforts to leave the valley, Rasselas becomes acquainted with the poet Imlac. Imlac has

travelled extensively through India, Persia, Arabia, and Europe
(chs. 8–12, pp. 347–58) and his observations have led him to the
conclusion that 'Human life is everywhere a state in which
much is to be endured and little to be enjoyed' (ch. 11, p. 355).
He agrees to help Rasselas in his escape and become 'the
companion of [his] flight, the guide of [his] rambles, the
partner of [his] fortune, and [his] sole director in the *choice of
life*' (ch. 12, p. 358). In the end, Rasselas leaves accompanied by
Imlac, his sister Princess Nekayah, and her maid Pekuah, and
the rest of the book follows the travels, adventures, and
philosophical speculations of these four.

Following their escape in chapter fifteen, the four travel to
Egypt, where the prince and princess begin their researches to
enable them to make their *'choice of life'* (ch. 16, p. 362). They
examine the lives of the rich and the poor, the idle and the
industrious, the philosopher and the peasant, in order to
ascertain how life can be lived in happiness and virtue. They
explore different kinds of philosophy, through meeting repre-
sentatives of the Stoic and Epicurean systems. But the pessimistic message of the book is reinforced, as time and again the
travellers think that they have found an individual who is wise
and happy and has discovered the answer to the question of
'how to live', only to be disappointed.

In a scene that echoes the satire on Parson Adams in Henry
Fielding's *Joseph Andrews*,[11] Rasselas is impressed by a philosopher who discourses on the importance of reason, and the
need to control the passions. The next day he finds the man
overwhelmed by grief, following the death of his daughter.
' "What comfort", said the mourner, "can truth and reason
afford me? of what effect are they now, but to tell me, that my
daughter will not be restored?" ' (ch. 18, pp. 365–7). As Imlac
comments, 'the teachers of morality . . . discourse like angels,
but they live like men' (ch. 18, p. 366).

The life of rural simplicity is represented as far from a
pastoral idyll. The shepherds are 'rude and ignorant' (ch. 19,
p. 367) and their hearts are 'cankered with discontent' (ch. 19,
p. 368). The rich man lives in permanent anxiety that he will
lose his property (ch. 20, pp. 368–9) while the hermit pines for
society (ch. 21, pp. 369–71). Nekayah's investigations into the
advisability of the married state produce the oft-quoted

observation that 'Marriage has many pains, but celibacy has no pleasures' (ch. 26, p. 377).

Following the discussion on marriage, Imlac tells Rasselas and Nekayah that, 'while you are making the choice of life, you neglect to live' (ch. 30, p. 383). This introduces the third section of the book, in which the pursuit of 'how to live' is abandoned without any conclusion being reached. The party goes off to visit the Great Pyramid, and this provides another opportunity for moral reflection, for Imlac regards this edifice as a monument to vanity and 'the insufficiency of human enjoyments':

> A king whose power is unlimited, and whose treasures surmount all real and imaginary wants, is compelled to solace, by the erection of a pyramid, the satiety of dominion and tastelessness of pleasures, and to amuse the tediousness of declining life, by seeing thousands labouring without end, and one stone, for no purpose, laid upon another. Whoever thou art that, not content with a moderate condition, imaginest happiness in royal magnificence, and dreamest that command or riches can feed the appetite of novelty with perpetual gratifications, survey the pyramids, and confess thy folly! (ch. 32, pp. 387–8)

Walter Jackson Bate has stressed the symbolic significance of Imlac's account of the 'hunger of imagination' that has led to the construction of the pyramids. This is the condition that afflicts all the characters in the book, and motivates their permanent state of restless searching.[12] The Great Pyramid can therefore be seen as a massive metaphor for the bleak vision of the human psyche that emerges from the text as a whole. Yet it is while Imlac, Rasselas, and Nekayah are inside the pyramid that the maid, Pekuah, is snatched away by a group of Arab horsemen. In the search for, and restitution of, Pekuah, Rasselas is forced to become an active participant in everyday life, instead of a passive spectator, surveying and judging from the outside.

Emrys Jones has argued that *Rasselas* is divided into three distinct sections, each comprising sixteen chapters. The first presents Rasselas's life in the Happy Valley, and the discontent that causes him to leave. The second section deals with the 'choice of life' question, as the travellers discover the problems involved in making rational decisions. The third section starts after the visit to the Great Pyramid, and describes Pekuah's abduction and the meeting with the astronomer. In this section, the formal quest is sidelined, as the travellers become more involved in life. Jones argues that the final, forty-ninth, chapter can be seen as a 'trailing coda', following but not resolving the preceding sections.[13]

Jones's reading is a little too schematic. After all, the travellers leave the valley in chapter fifteen, so chapter sixteen would seem to be the first chapter in the second section rather than the last in the first. But the framework of a tripartite division highlights the significant shifts that take place in the narrative. After the return of Pekuah, however, the narrative becomes concerned with the story of the astronomer, which can be read as a further contribution to the choice of life debate of the second section.

The astronomer is presented as a man of learning, wisdom, and courtesy. He appears to have found the answer to the great question of 'how to live', yet he seems to labour under a secret sorrow. He eventually confides to Imlac the source of his grief, which is that he believes himself to be responsible for 'the regulation of the weather and the distribution of the seasons'. He tells Imlac that for five years:

> The sun has listened to my dictates, and passed from tropic to tropic by my direction; the clouds, at my call, have poured their waters, and the Nile has overflowed at my command; I have restrained the rage of the dog-star, and mitigated the fervours of the crab. The winds alone, of all the elemental powers, have hitherto refused my authority, and multitudes have perished in equinoctial tempests which I found myself unable to prohibit or restrain. (ch. 41, p. 403)

Some critics have related the portrayal of the astronomer's mania to Johnson's fears for his own intellect. He always felt that the gap between sanity and insanity was for him, at least, worryingly narrow, and the travellers in *Rasselas* draw a direct connection between disorder of the intellect and the exercise of the imagination. The indulgence of fancy, or 'the power of fiction', is portrayed as a dangerous occupation, because it can make you lose touch with the more prosaic realities of the physical world. Pekuah, Nekayah, and Rasselas therefore vow that they will no longer occupy themselves with visionary schemes or waking dreams (ch. 44, p. 406). But whereas the encounters with the various exemplary figures in the second section last only as long as it takes to derive the moral lesson of the meeting, the relationship with the astronomer is developed in the final section of the book, as he becomes a significant character. After initial amusement at his delusion, Pekuah and Nekayah become anxious to make the acquaintance of one 'at once so amiable and so strange' (ch. 46, p. 409) and arrange a meeting under the pretext that Pekuah wishes to develop her knowledge of astronomy. Despite Imlac's warning that 'he will be soon weary of your company' since 'men advanced far in knowledge do not love to repeat the elements of their art' (ch. 46, p. 410), the contrary proves to be the case. The two women make repeated visits to the astronomer and are 'every time more welcome than before' (ch. 46, p. 411).

While Pekuah and Nekayah develop their astronomical knowledge, the astronomer also learns and changes, through visiting the friends and acquiring the social arts of conversation and conviviality. He 'came early and departed late' and 'laboured to recommend himself by assiduity and compliance', so that, when the prince and his sister finally consult him on the old question of 'the choice of life', he can only inform them that he himself has 'chosen wrong'. His dedication to study has ensured that he has 'missed the endearing elegance of female friendship, and the happy commerce of domestic tenderness' (ch. 46, p. 411). The 'familiar friendship' of the travellers and the daily programme of 'projects and pleasures' gradually weakens the power of his delusion, so that he begins to doubt whether he really has been given the task of controlling the weather.

If *Rasselas* were a standard eighteenth-century novel, we could imagine that it would end with the marriage of Pekuah and the astronomer, as a confirmation of her reclamation of him from the madness that has been shown to be consequent on isolated study and avoidance of the company and diversions of the social world. Yet nothing of the kind happens. The final chapter is entitled 'The conclusion, in which nothing is concluded'. The friends discuss their wishes for the future, but they 'well knew that none could be obtained'. They therefore 'deliberated a while what was to be done, and resolved . . . to return to Abyssinia' (ch. 49, p. 418). Again, if this were a conventional novel, we would want to know how Rasselas intended to evade the punishment due for his escape from the Happy Valley. But this is not a conventional novel. The title of the final chapter draws attention to the absence of narrative closure, and this reflects the lack of philosophical closure.

The ending of the narrative seems to uphold the words of Rasselas that 'The more we enquire, the less we can resolve' (ch. 26, p. 377). There is no answer to the question of 'the choice of life', or even to Nekayah's redefinition of the question as 'the choice of eternity' (ch. 48, p. 418). Nothing is decided about the issues of whether the individual should marry or stay celibate; mix in the world, or retreat into solitude or a religious community; devote him or herself to study or to the pleasures of social or domestic felicity. The 'quest' that has formed the basic structural principle of much of the book is simply abandoned, as the friends decide the grail is not worth pursuing and go home.

The inconclusiveness of the ending can be read as a challenge to Enlightenment notions of rationality, and the idea that all questions must have an answer. But it also seems to undermine the figure of Imlac, who is characterized as a devotee of reason. His sentiments are conveyed in pithy precepts that seem to remove all scope for doubt. We are told that 'he that lives well cannot be despised' (ch. 26, p. 377); that 'Example is always more efficacious than precept' (ch. 30, p. 385), and that 'He that lives well in the world is better than he that lives well in a monastery' (ch. 47, p. 414). The authoritative tone of Imlac's words, and the formulation of his views as sayings or aphorisms, have encouraged both critics and readers to share the perspective of Rasselas, Nekayah, and Pekuah, who tend to lap up his words as truths that are beyond question. He is conventionally associated with Johnson, who was similarly given to aphoristic assertion.[14]

At the end of the book, these three friends express their hopes and desires for the future. Pekuah wants to be prioress to a convent of pious maidens. Nekayah wants to found a college of learned women, and Rasselas desires to be the just monarch of a little kingdom. In contrast to these worthy aspirations, Imlac and the astronomer, the apparent moral guides, 'were contented to be driven along the stream of life without directing their course to any particular port'. But, ironically, it is this aim that is immediately undermined, for in the end they all resolve 'to return to Abyssinia', which would inevitably mean directing their course to a particular port. This final satirical note suggests some subversion of the authority of Imlac and a challenge to his sententious utterances. At the least, caution must be exerted in accepting his pronouncements at face value, and readers should beware of any straightforward assimilation of the views of Imlac with those of Johnson himself. In the end, Imlac cannot provide an answer to the central questions. Even the great poet and philosopher is left in a state of doubt and uncertainty, which ultimately seems to represent Johnson's view of human life.

Rasselas therefore embodies the Johnsonian preoccupation with literary sermonizing in the wise words of Imlac, yet it also challenges the notion of authorial didacticism in the absence of philosophical closure and the ironic undermining of its sententious moral guide. While narrative expectations are frustrated by the absence of any kind of denouement, the didactic purpose is subverted by the refusal to provide an adequate answer to the fundamental questions posed. Although passing reference is made to 'the choice of eternity', the abiding impression derived from the narrative is of a world devoid of spiritual consolation and replete with a sense of human misery. Imlac refers to 'him by whose laws our actions are governed, and who will suffer none to be finally punished for obedience' (ch. 34, p. 390), but there is no sense that this concept of a first cause or god is underpinned by revelation. Thus, by setting his tale outside the Christian world, Johnson is able to give free rein to his pessimistic view of the human condition and present human nature as inherently dissatisfied, and discontent and disappointment as inescapable features of the human lot.

Rasselas therefore constructs a rather different image of human nature from that of *The Vanity of Human Wishes*. The characters in *Vanity* think that they know what they want; they just do not like it when they get it. The characters in *Rasselas* do not know what they want in the first place. Moreover, *Vanity* suggests that human happiness is ultimately achievable, through an appeal to 'celestial wisdom', which can furnish us with 'a healthful mind, | Obedient passions, and a will resigned' (Vanity, ll. 359–60).[15]

Fred Parker had emphasized the importance of *Rasselas* as a manifestation of Johnson's scepticism, seeing the text as 'a point of vantage from which to appreciate the coherence and interconnectedness of his whole thought'.[16] He identifies an underlying tension between, on the one hand, Johnson's 'power of aphoristic compression',[17] which leads to the construction of homilies that imply the existence of a stable moral system and a state of philosophical certainty, and, on the other, a sense of uncertainty that highlights the difficulty of providing clear answers to moral questions.

As a philosophical tale, *Rasselas* has always invited comparison with *Candide* by Voltaire, which was published in January 1759, only three months before Johnson's work came out. *Candide* does not have a specifically Eastern location, for its characters journey all over the world. Moreover, its tone is consistently comic and satiric and, although Fred Parker has made a good case for the 'wit' of *Rasselas*, no one has seriously suggested that it is actually funny. Nonetheless, there are striking similarities between the themes and content of the two texts. Candide's experience of suffering and injustice challenges the view repeatedly expressed by his syphilitic tutor and philosopher, Pangloss, that 'everything is for the best' in this 'best of all possible worlds'.[18] Even when Candide and his servant, Cacambo, visit the magical land of Eldorado, where everything does seem to be for the best, they cannot be content. They continue to aspire to something beyond what they have, and have to make their escape, just as Rasselas has to flee from the Happy Valley. Both tales therefore underline the inevitability of suffering, but also that human nature is inherently unsatisfied. We will always strive for something we cannot achieve, for without this our lives will be meaningless. They therefore challenge the creed of philosophical optimism, which Voltaire presents as a cloak for callous indifference and resistance to social change.

At the end of Voltaire's tale, Candide and his group of friends retire to Turkey, where, as the pessimistic scholar Martin declares, they 'must work without arguing' because 'that is the only way to make life bearable'.[19] So, while *Rasselas* ends with the decision to return to Abyssinia, *Candide* ends with the words of its hero, 'we must go and work in the garden'.[20] There are no ideal solutions to the problems of the world. All we can do is make the most of what we have got and get on with the business of life. In each of these philosophical tales, therefore, philosophy is shown to be a pointless pursuit.

Rasselas could also be compared with a work such as Henry Fielding's *Tom Jones*, in that this novel is also concerned with the question of 'how to live'. Both works deal with issues of marriage, career, and social morality, in order to ascertain how men and women can live virtuously in the modern world. Fielding explores these issues by creating a recognizable character, with whom readers can identify, whose trials and experiences are similar to those that readers may encounter in their own lives. In contrast, Johnson constructs an exotic Abyssinian setting that is clearly outside the experience of his readers. The perfect Happy Valley is drawn from the realm of myth or fairy tale, rather than the real world. In this respect, Johnson appears to be locating his tale as far as possible from the conventional, recognizable world of the novel. While the location may draw on the popularity of the Oriental Tale, the narrative voice ironically celebrates its lack of traditional plot mechanisms and fictional closure.

Rasselas is therefore a prose narrative, written for the market, which resists identification with the novel, the form that has been identified as characteristic of the developing commercial society. For Johnson, recognition of the economic potential of the expanding readership and new technological developments was qualified by a residual uncertainty about the implications of these changes for the development of literary genres and the relationship between writer and reader. As *Rambler* 4 makes clear, Johnson was reluctant to accept the empiricist emphasis of the novel, with the prioritization of the reader's interpretative role. He was preoccupied with moral and preceptual forms, such as the periodical essay, and, despite his need to write for the market, he believed the primary purpose of literature was to convey moral instruction. Fiction is associated in *Rasselas* with potentially dangerous delusions that may lead us to lose sight of our place in the real world.

Yet Johnson clearly had his finger on the pulse of the mid-eighteenth-century market. Despite the bleakness of its moral vision, *Rasselas* proved extremely popular and successful, selling 3,500 copies in its first year. Initial critical reactions were mixed, however. While most reviewers recognized the worthiness of the tale, some were troubled by the attempt to present a philosophical treatise in the guise of a prose romance. The reviewer for the *Critical Review* commented:

> Upon the whole, we imagine the talents of the author would appear to more advantage, had he treated his different subjects in the method of essays, or form of dialogue. At present, the title page will, by many readers, be looked upon as a decoy, to deceive them into a kind of knowledge they had no inclination to be acquainted with.[21]

In an unsigned review in the *Monthly Review*, Owen Ruffhead developed a similar argument, observing 'of the learned writer of these volumes': 'That *tale-telling* evidently is not his talent. He wants that graceful ease, which is the ornament of romance; and he stalks in the solemn buskin, when he ought to tread in the light sock.'[22] Like the *Critical*, he believes that the tale is calculated to mislead the customers of the circulating library, 'who, while they expect to frolic along the flowery paths of romance, will find themselves hoisted on metaphysical stilts, and born aloft into the regions of syllogistic subtlety, and philosophical refinement'.[23]

These criticisms are significant because they suggest that there is a growing sense of what the form and content of a prose romance should be, and that the subversion of these expectations is seen as dishonest or fraudulent. While prose fiction conventionally begins with a reference to the potential of the form to inculcate moral lessons, the readers do not expect the kind of weighty didacticism that *Rasselas* contains. For 'the young, the ignorant and the idle' readers of the mid-eighteenth century, the 'choice of life' could be more palatably explored through the adventures of Miss Betsy Thoughtless or Tom Jones than through the elevated debates of Imlac and Rasselas.

5

Shakespeare and the *Prefaces*

THE WORKS OF SHAKESPEARE

Rasselas was represented as the product of an intensive burst of inspired creativity, but its composition occurred while Johnson was engaged in a much larger and characteristically tortuous project, from which the philosophical tale may have formed a refreshing change. This was an edition of *The Plays of William Shakespeare in Eight Volumes, with the Corrections and Illustrations of Various Commentators; To which are added Notes by Sam. Johnson*, which Johnson prepared for the press, writing extensive annotations to explain the meaning of particular words or lines, and providing concluding notes to give a general account and criticism of each of the plays. These notes bring out the themes, the beauties, and any technical or moral problems that Johnson perceived in the work. The publication history of this ambitious edition echoes the tale of the compilation of the *Dictionary*. In both cases the work was heralded in advance, but then years elapsed before it reached completion. Both were ideas that had been at the back of Johnson's mind for a considerable period.

In 1745 Johnson brought out his *Miscellaneous Observations on the Tragedy of Macbeth*, with a proposal for a new edition of the plays. This plan was abandoned, probably partly in response to pressure from the publisher of a rival edition, and was then resurrected in 1756 with the production of the lengthy *Proposals for Printing the Dramatick Works of William Shakespeare*. This outlined Johnson's plans and editorial principles, and set down the following 'Conditions' as a form of advertisement to attract subscribers to the project. Johnson assured his readers:

I. That the book shall be elegantly printed in eight volumes in octavo.

II. That the price to subscribers shall be two guineas; one to be paid at subscribing, the other on the delivery of the book in sheets.

III. That the work shall be published on or before Christmas 1757. (*Works*, vii. 58)

Publication by subscription was often used in the eighteenth century to ease the financial burden of getting a work into print. Proposals would be circulated prior to publication outlining the nature of the work. Interested individuals could then make a contribution towards the cost of production and commit themselves to buying the finished book. In return they would have their names listed in the final 'elegantly printed' volume, enabling them to gain some status as patrons of the arts, but at fairly minimal cost. This system of publication has been seen as an important transitional phase between the aristocratic patronage of the Renaissance and the purely commercial publication of the nineteenth century. Terry Eagleton suggests that it was a process 'which converted readers into collective patrons and transformed their otherwise passive, "nuclear" relation to the text into membership of a community of benevolent participants in the writing project'.[1] By being involved in the publication, reasonably affluent individuals could be encouraged to become part of the public sphere, and would also have an interest in ensuring that the final volume was heralded as a success.

In response to the *Proposals*, subscribers duly came forward to support Johnson's venture, but these benevolent participants had to be extremely patient. Far from being out by Christmas 1757, it was 1765 before the edition finally appeared, and the protracted delay produced some mockery in periodicals such as the *Critical Review* and the *Monthly Review*.[2] As with the *Dictionary*, the delay was a consequence of a combination of Johnson's natural indolence, his involvement in other projects (including, of course, *Rasselas* and the *Idler*), and the sheer enormity of the task involved. Walter Jackson Bate has argued that the years of the preparation of the *Shakespeare* were the time of Johnson's greatest struggle against encroaching insanity.[3] It is in this light that Bate interprets the padlock that was in the possession of Johnson's intimate friend Mrs Thrale and labelled 'Johnson's padlock, committed to my care in 1768'. Bate argues that Johnson kept the padlock so that he could be restrained if his mania ever became unmanageable, although other commentators have suggested that this instrument of bondage may have had some kind of sexual significance (DeMaria, 260–1).[4]

Robert DeMaria sees the *Shakespeare* project as a direct consequence of Johnson's work on the *Dictionary*, which had given him an intimate acquaintance with Shakespeare's plays. In the late 1740s he had read through the complete works 'and marked out over 20,000 words, the meanings of which he found well illustrated in their Shakespearian contexts' (De-Maria, 218–19). DeMaria suggests that both the *Dictionary* and the *Shakespeare* should be seen to belong 'to the same series of projects on the history of learning'. They represent Johnson's increasing acceptance that the focus of literature and scholarship could no longer be the classics of Latin and Greek. Furthermore, classical standards and classical ideals did not always provide the most appropriate criteria for the evaluation of modern, vernacular literature and modern society. Johnson was therefore increasingly involved in literary projects concerned with the refinement of English language and culture. DeMaria argues that 'although Johnson always maintained a private conversation with classical learning, in his published works the trajectory of his drive to produce scholarship akin to that of his classicist idols is largely downward, from classical aspirations to merely English, and from vastly ambitious projects to more narrow achievements' (DeMaria, 219). Johnson's retreat from classicism is here presented as a narrative of defeat and pessimistic resignation, as the great scholar recognized the inapplicability of his classical heroes within a contemporary context. Yet it is possible to see this change of focus in more positive terms, as part of a growing appreciation of the value and power of the English literature in which Johnson had been immersed during his work on the *Dictionary*. The public retreat from the classics, manifested, for instance, in the change in Johnson's attitude towards the genre of poetic imitation,[5] may also represent the emergence of a more inclusive concept of the reading public and its relationship to literature. While early works such as *London* and *The Vanity of Human Wishes* consciously exploited the exclusivity that resulted from their reliance on classical models, the *Shakespeare* sought to make its subject available to a wide readership, through the provision of extensive explanatory notes.

To the modern reader Johnson's notes may not always seem an aid to interpretation. They frequently manifest a combative critical spirit, engaging in debate with, or derision of, other Shakespeare editors. But they indicate a significant desire to make the text accessible, and show Johnson's recognition of the discriminatory abilities of the readership, as well as his desire to highlight and clarify the moral message of particular passages. In the notes to *Measure for Measure*, for example, the Duke's observation in Act III, Scene i, that 'all th'accommodations, that thou bear'st, | Are nurs'd by baseness', is glossed in a note that first engages with the critic William Warburton's earlier interpretation of the lines, but then analyses the sentiment expressed on the grounds of moral and rational rather than purely textual or literary reasoning. Johnson asserts that:

> Dr *Warburton* is undoubtedly mistaken in supposing that by *baseness* is meant *self-love* here assigned as the motive of all human actions. *Shakespeare* meant only to observe that a minute analysis of life at once destroys that splendour which dazzles the imagination. Whatever grandeur can display, or luxury enjoy, is procured by *baseness*, by offices of which the mind shrinks from the contemplation. All the delicacies of the table may be traced back to the shambles and the dunghill, all magnificence of building was hewn from the quarry, and all the pomp of ornaments, dug from among the damps and darkness of the mine.   (Greene, 458)

We, as readers, are given guidance in relation to the meaning of the speech, but the argument appeals to our knowledge and experience of the world. It is assumed that we will recognize the truth of the observation that great or beautiful things may have humble origins, whereas we must see that the argument that baseness should be interpreted as human selfishness cannot be true because this perspective is not morally acceptable. Johnson cannot believe that Shakespeare would use the Duke to articulate the philosophy that human behaviour is purely selfish, and therefore takes it for granted that there must be a different interpretation.

Moral arguments likewise inform Johnson's verdicts in his concluding comments on the plays. He praises *King Lear* as 'deservedly celebrated', claiming that 'there is perhaps no play which keeps the attention so strongly fixed; which so much agitates our passions and interests our curiosity' (Greene, 463). Nonetheless he has difficulty with the 'extrusion of Glouces- ter's eyes, which seems an act too horrid to be endured in dramatic exhibition' (Greene, 464), and also with the death of Cordelia. Johnson's primary reaction to this event is emotional. He tells us that 'I was many years ago so shocked by Cordelia's death that I know not whether I ever endured to read again the last scenes of the play till I undertook to revise them as editor' (Greene, 465). But once again his aesthetic judgement is based on moral principles. For:

> A play in which the wicked prosper, and the virtuous miscarry, may doubtless be good, because it is a just representation of the common events of human life: but since all reasonable beings naturally love justice, I cannot easily be persuaded that the observation of justice makes a play worse; or, that if other excellencies are equal, the audience will not always rise better pleased from the final triumph of persecuted virtue. (Greene, 465)

When the complete edition of *The Plays of William Shakespeare* finally came out, the annotated text was preceded by a preface, justifying the work by an analysis of the source of Shake- speare's poetic power, and a defence of his plays against the criticisms most commonly levelled. The preface has been seen as an important statement of Johnson's critical philosophy and a contribution to the eighteenth-century debate over the nature and function of criticism. Some commentators have interpreted it as a manifestation of Johnson's continued adherence to traditional 'neoclassical' ideas of literature,[6] but others have seen it as more modern.[7] One of the assertions in the preface that has received extensive consideration is Johnson's state- ment that 'nothing can please many, and please long, but just representations of general nature' (Greene, 420). He goes on to argue that 'Shakespeare is above all writers, at least above all modern writers, the poet of nature; the poet that holds up to his readers a faithfull mirror of manners and life' (Greene, 421). This emphasis on nature, and on literature as a mirror that reflects nature and life, has been seen as a manifestation of Johnson's 'rich humanism'.[8] Yet it is important to bear in mind that Johnson is not using the term 'nature' in quite the same way that we would use it today. Johnson locates the source of Shakespeare's creative power in the fact that he does not represent characters that are 'modified by the customs of particular places'. Instead his creations 'are the genuine progeny of common humanity' (Greene, 421). This suggests a platonic rather than a realist concept of 'nature'. In Johnson's view, authors should represent universal types rather than particular individuals. They should be not stereotypes, but archetypes, which embody the essence of character. Johnson argues that 'in the writings of other poets a character is too often an individual; in those of Shakespeare it is commonly a species' and it is clear that this is a strong tribute to Shakespeare's literary power. His view of the poet's function is therefore comparable to that expressed by Imlac in *Rasselas*:

> The business of a poet . . . is to examine, not the individual, but the species; to remark general properties and large appearances: he does not number the streaks of the tulip, or describe the different shades in the verdure of the forest. He is to exhibit in his portraits of nature such prominent and striking features as recall the original to every mind.   (ch. 10, p. 352)

Johnson's nature is therefore an essentially classical concept. It is very different from the emphasis on rounded individuals that was to develop within the novel, and that has inspired much anachronistic criticism of the characterization within eighteenth-century fiction. Although Johnson frequently attacked the works of Henry Fielding, the two writers seem to have been using comparable neoclassical concepts of character and nature. In the preface to *Joseph Andrews* Fielding's narrator remarks that he will confine himself strictly to Nature, 'from the just Imitation of which, will flow all the Pleasure we can this way convey to a sensible Reader'.[9] He goes on to explain in the introductory chapter to book three, in anticipation of accusations that his portraits represent attacks on real people, that 'I describe not Men, but Manners; not an Individual, but a Species'. His aim is 'to hold the Glass to thousands in their closets'.[10]

Johnson dismisses the criticism that Shakespeare's Romans are not sufficiently Roman on the grounds that 'a poet overlooks the casual distinction of country and condition, as a painter, satisfied with the figure, neglects the drapery' (Greene, 423). Fielding's narrator similarly compares the 'little Circumstances' of characterization with 'the Drapery of a Picture, which tho' Fashion varies at different Times, the Resemblance of the Countenance is not by those means diminished'.[11] For both Johnson and Fielding the essence of character portrayal was the presentation of essential features, not the portrayal of incidental details of dress or appearance that may vary over time. The *Dictionary* includes the following definitions of 'character':

4. A representation of any man as to his personal qualities.
Each drew fair *characters*, yet none
Of these they feign'd excels their own. *Denham*
Homer has excelled all the heroick poets that ever wrote, in the multitude and variety of his *characters*; every god that is admitted into his poem, acts a part which would have been suitable to no other deity. *Addison*
6. The person with his assemblage of qualities; a personage.
In a tragedy, or epick poem, the hero of the piece must be advanced foremost to the view of the reader or spectator; he must outshine the rest of all the *characters*; he must appear the prince of them, like the sun in the Copernican system, encompassed with the less noble planets. *Dryden*[12]

These two definitions develop the specifically literary aspects of character, but each is illustrated with references to classical, epic models. Combined with Johnson's preoccupation with the timelessness of dramatic characterization, they suggest an adherence to neoclassical concepts of literary form that can be related to the earlier comments on linguistic propriety in *Rambler* 168, in which Johnson expressed his dislike of Shakespeare's use of 'low' words.

Elsewhere in the preface the terms of the defence of Shakespeare indicate a willingness to depart from the rules derived from the classical texts, or, at least, to interpret them

71

more liberally than was the case in the prevalent neoclassical tradition. For example, many eighteenth-century critics drew on the arguments of Aristotle's *Poetics* to support the idea that drama was divided into tragedy and comedy and that these two forms had their own distinct conventions. From this developed the concept of a rigid hierarchy of literary genres and critical strictures that all works should conform to one of the prescribed categories. By the mid-eighteenth century this belief that tragic and comic drama should be wholly distinct had become a fundamental axiom of neoclassicism, perhaps emphasized all the more strongly because of a conscious or unconscious recognition that these boundaries were becoming increasingly blurred within the emergent form of the novel. But in the preface Johnson defends Shakespeare against accusations that his works violated literary rules through their promiscuous mixing of comic and tragic elements and the defence appeals to our own experience of life. Johnson suggests that Shakespeare's plays are 'not in the rigorous and critical sense either tragedies or comedies, but compositions of a distinct kind; exhibiting the real state of sublunary nature, which partakes of good and evil, joy and sorrow, mingled with endless variety of proportion and innumerable modes of combination' (Greene, 423). Life is not divided into tragedy and comedy. Our knowledge of the world tells us that good and evil are mixed up together and Johnson suggests that this should be reflected within drama. 'That this is a practice contrary to the rules of criticism will be readily allowed; but there is always an appeal open from criticism to nature'. Critical strictures may be over ruled by reference to experience of life and thus Johnson suggests that the views of the ordinary reader can be used to challenge the theories advocated by the professional critic. For Johnson, as for Fielding, the professional critic may be the reader who is most likely to misinterpret the text, because he may be blinded by his preconceptions and theories.

Johnson also addresses the criticism that had been levelled against Shakespeare on the grounds that he failed to adhere to the unities of time and place. In his *Poetics* Aristotle had laid down 'General Principles' for the composition of tragedy. He stated that the action of the plot 'ought to be both unified and complete, and the component events ought to be so firmly compacted that if any one of them is shifted to another place, or removed, the whole is loosened up and dislocated'.[13] In neoclassical criticism this principle developed into the concept of the 'unities'. It was argued that drama should not violate probability, and therefore that its action should be single, not complex, and occur in one place and over a limited period of time. Johnson argues that adherence to the unities derives from a desire for credibility:

> The critics hold it impossible that an action of months or years can be possibly believed to pass in three hours; or that the spectator can suppose himself to sit in the theatre, while ambassadors go and return between distant kings, while armies are levied and towns are besieged, while an exile wanders and returns, or till he whom they saw courting his mistress shall lament the untimely fall of his son. (Greene, 430)

But in response to this theory Johnson claims that, when we go to watch a play, we do not actually believe ourselves to be in the place in which the drama is set. We do not think that our walk to the theatre has taken us to Egypt, and that we live in the days of Anthony and Cleopatra. 'The truth is', Johnson asserts, 'that the spectators are always in their senses, and know, from the first act to the last, that the stage is only a stage, and that the players are only players' (Greene, 431). This may seem obvious to modern readers, but Johnson extends the argument to challenge the concept of the unities of time and place that was central to the neoclassical creed. The play presents a particular action or event but 'the different actions that complete a story may be in places very remote from each other; and where is the absurdity of allowing that space to represent first Athens, and then Sicily, which was always known to be neither Sicily nor Athens, but a modern theatre?' (Greene, 431).

The audience can imagine themselves in one place, and then in another, so that unity of place is not required to maintain the credibility of a dramatic representation. In the same way, they can imagine that time has passed between one action and another, for 'a lapse of years is as easily conceived as a passage of hours' (Greene, 431–2), so that unity of time is likewise unnecessary.

Johnson argues that drama works as 'a just picture of a real original', but it should never be confused with that original. 'The delight of tragedy proceeds from our consciousness of fiction', for we would not enjoy witnessing wars and murders if we believed them to be real. Thus 'Imitations produce pain or pleasure, not because they are mistaken for realities, but because they bring realities to mind' (Greene, 432). We are able to experience events vicariously, and consider how we would react in comparable circumstances, without having to undergo any of the dangers or difficulties involved. So, in drawing on Aristotle's concept that art is an imitation of nature, Johnson emphasizes the importance of nature as the subject of drama, but he also stresses the need for the audience to recognize that what they are seeing is a representation, and not to be confused with the reality. The preface, like the annotations to the plays, is couched in a tone of appeal to the reason and reactions of the readers and spectators of Shakespeare's text. While neoclassicism saw literary criticism in terms of a set of codes and conventions handed down from antiquity, articulated by critical authorities, and used as a standard against which works could be measured, Johnson is more concerned to assess the impact of works upon an audience. If a play does not obey the unities of time and place, or if it combines elements of tragedy and comedy, it should not be condemned purely on the basis of some abstract theory. Such transgressions are significant only if they impede the pleasure or understanding of those watching or reading, or undermine their belief that the play is an imitation of nature. Indeed, following his analysis of Shakespeare's neglect of the unities, Johnson goes so far as to satirize the whole idea of dramatic rules, arguing that 'a play written with nice observation of critical rules is to be contemplated as an elaborate curiosity, as the product of superfluous and ostentatious art, by which is shown rather what is possible than what is necessary' (Greene, 433). As Walter Jackson Bate suggests, the tenor of the preface is that 'If the neo-classic rules of the drama conflict with the achievement of Shakespeare, it is they that are inadequate, not Shakespeare'.[14] The preface therefore seems to hinge on the assumption that the audience for drama is endowed with powers of discrimination far greater than were implicit in neoclassical criticism, and also considerably more than were credited to the readers of fiction in *Rambler* 4.

THE PREFACES TO THE WORKS OF THE ENGLISH POETS

Johnson's reputation as one of the founders of the discipline of literary criticism is based on his periodical essays, his *Shakespeare*, and also his last literary project, often now known as the *Lives of the Poets*. The impetus for this project probably came from the booksellers, who wanted to bring out a series of volumes containing selections from famous poets. Johnson's role was to provide a short preface to each one, giving a biographical sketch and an introduction to the works contained in the volume. Thus the *Lives* were originally entitled *Prefaces to the Works of the English Poets*. The choice of which poets were to be included was made by the publishers and was based on the need to maintain the copyright on a number of authors from the relatively recent past, rather than purely aesthetic concerns. This undermines the arguments of literary critics who have cited the selection of poets in the *Prefaces* as evidence of Johnson's neoclassicism, and his preoccupation with work from the period after Milton. By the time the full series appeared in 1781, however, Johnson's prefaces had grown too long to be included within the volumes to which they referred, and were instead printed together. The series was finally made up of sixty-eight octavo volumes: fifty-six of poetry, ten of prefaces, and two of index.

Each of the fifty-two prefaces follows roughly the same format, with a biography of the poet, an evaluation of his character, and then criticism of the works. This tripartite structure had been used in 'Lives' by earlier writers,[15] and after Johnson it became the standard format for literary biography. What most immediately strikes the modern reader is the judiciousness with which Johnson evaluates both character and verse. He presents the positive and negative aspects of each, before weighing them up in his final assessment. While he praises the character of William Collins as a friend with whom he once delighted to converse, and whom he remembers with tenderness, his judgement of his poetry is more censorious. We are informed that 'his diction was often harsh, unskilfully laboured, and injudiciously selected. He affected the obsolete when it was not worthy of revival; and he puts his words out of the common order, seeming to think, with some later candidates for fame, that not to write prose is certainly to write poetry' (Greene, 761). The criticism is not merely an *ad hoc* response to the individual poets, however. Certain themes recur, as Johnson develops his standards and criteria, and also celebrates the work of previous critics such as Dryden.

One of his most famous and influential literary verdicts occurs in his first preface, the 'Life of Cowley', where Johnson uses Dryden's term 'Metaphysical Poets' to refer to the 'race of writers' that appeared in the early seventeenth century. While Johnson has been censured for his critique, particularly after the revival of interest in the metaphysicals in the twentieth century, he made an important contribution to the study of their verse by labelling and defining the genre. He suggests that the characteristic feature of metaphysical verse is its use of 'conceits' in which 'the most heterogeneous ideas are yoked by violence together'. A diverse range of imagery is utilized, so that 'nature and art are ransacked for illustrations, comparisons, and allusions'. Thus, although we may find, when we look at the work of the metaphysical poets, that 'their learning instructs, and their subtlety surprises', nonetheless the disjunction of ideas is such that 'the reader commonly thinks his improvement dearly bought, and, though he sometimes admires, is seldom pleased' (Greene, 678). Johnson's critique is based on the claim that these writers tend to indulge in a 'voluntary deviation from nature in pursuit of something new and strange'. They therefore 'fail to give delight by their desire of exciting admiration' (Greene, 687).

The comments on both Collins and Cowley reveal an underlying concern with nature as the fundamental basis of literary judgements. The poetry of Collins is censured for departing from nature in its artificially archaic diction. Metaphysical writers such as John Donne and Ben Jonson are criticized for their unnatural imagery and for having 'neither copied nature nor life' (Greene, 677). Yet, while Johnson's 'Cowley' has frequently been represented as a savage attack on the metaphysical poets, the final verdict is not entirely negative. With his customary even-handedness Johnson recognized that 'great labour directed by great abilities is never wholly lost'. So, if the metaphysical writers 'frequently threw away their wit upon false conceits, they likewise sometimes struck out unexpected truth; if their conceits were far fetched, they were often worth the carriage' (Greene, 679). His personal interest in these writings is indicated in the inclusion of over a thousand citations from metaphysical writers in the *Dictionary*, many of which were quoted from memory.

In his life of John Milton, Johnson broke away from the rigid neoclassicism of earlier critics who had argued that *Paradise Lost* could not be considered an epic because it did not conform to epic rules of composition. It did not have a hero, and it lacked unity of action. Johnson argued that:

> The questions whether the action of the poem be strictly *one*, whether the poem can be properly termed *heroic*, and who is the hero, are raised by such readers as draw their principles of judgement rather from books than from reason ... Dryden, petulantly and indecently, denies the heroism of Adam because he was overcome; but there is no reason why the hero should not be unfortunate except established practice, since success and virtue do not necessarily go together.   (Greene, 706)

The assertion that Dryden acted 'petulantly and indecently' in refusing to recognize Adam as a hero because he was beaten suggests that literary criticism should be underlain by notions of fair play and good sportsmanship. The valiant loser can be an appropriate hero for modern times. Johnson therefore stressed the epic qualities of *Paradise Lost*, but in doing so he showed that flexibility was required in applying rules derived from the classics to works produced in a Christian society. Indeed Johnson argues that *Paradise Lost* is a superior poem because it deals with a Christian story rather than figures from classical history or mythology:

> The ancient epic poets, wanting the light of Revelation, were very unskilful teachers of virtue: their principal characters may be great, but they are not amiable. The reader may rise from their works with a greater degree of active or passive fortitude, and sometimes of prudence; but he will be able to carry away few precepts of justice, and none of mercy.   (Greene, 708)

He therefore maintained the critical approach of the preface to *Shakespeare* in that he accepted the importance of classical tradition, but rejected the use of classical models as a strait-jacket to confine vernacular works. He also developed this approach to suggest how the best aspects of modern society (that is, Christianity) could be used to inject new life into old forms.

While in his earliest poetic imitations, Johnson made his readers think by adapting old works to new circumstances, so his criticism in the *Prefaces* emphasized novelty and originality as crucial measures of literary merit. The metaphysicals are valued for their unexpected truths and unusual perspective, whereas the genre of pastoral is attacked as formulaic, irrelevant to modern life, and unlikely to generate anything new. But there is an increasing acceptance in the *Prefaces* that, although classical models have a crucial influence on literary form, writers cannot assume extensive classical knowledge on the part of 'common readers' (Greene, 750). Taken with his *Dictionary* and *Shakespeare*, the *Prefaces* represented Johnson's recognition of an autonomous vernacular tradition in which the common reader can be an active and discerning participant. This tradition can shape the moral values of its readers, but is also shaped by the morals and lives of those who have contributed to its construction. It is for this reason that it is fitting that Johnson's last great work should be the *Prefaces*, which draw on the interdependence of life and literature. Walter Jackson Bate indicates the intimate relationship between the analysis of life and work in Johnson's world view. He suggests that the prefaces are 'biography turning into criticism, not criticism withdrawing into biography. But neither would have seemed exclusive. The interest in either case is in informing and supplementing human experience.'[16]

6

A Journey to the Western Isles

On 6th August 1773 Johnson set out for Scotland, to join James Boswell on a long projected tour of the Highlands and Islands of Boswell's native land. Starting in Edinburgh, the pair travelled up the East Coast, via St Andrews, Montrose, and Aberdeen. They continued around the coast to Inverness and then across to the West Coast, taking in the islands of Skye, Coll, and Mull. Then they turned South along the West Coast, to visit Loch Lomond and the Boswell family home at Auchinlek, before returning to Edinburgh. The tour lasted three months, over rugged terrain in often inclement Scottish weather.

Johnson passed his sixty-fourth birthday in the course of the journey, a cumbersome, ageing, and often ailing man, yet he rose to the challenges of the hardships encountered, sleeping in hay when Boswell sought the comfort of sheets, venturing down caves and up precipices, and bouncing uncomfortably along on the small Highland ponies. Up to this point, most of his adult life had been passed in London, with only occasional visits to friends in Oxford or Lichfield. He had famously defended his lack of experience of the wider world on the grounds that 'there is in London all that Life can afford' (*Life*, 859). The Scottish tour heralded a new, more adventurous phase. In 1774 he accompanied his friends the Thrales on a tour of North Wales, and in 1775 he went with them on a trip to Paris.

In the course of the Scottish tour, Boswell despatched a series of articles to the *Caledonian Mercury* giving accounts of the progress of the pair. These were reprinted in other Scottish papers, and the journey became something of a news event.

This was in part because of Johnson's age, infirmities, and intellectual fame, which lent incongruity to the image of him travelling across such wild terrain. Boswell begins his account of the tour, *The Journal of a Tour to the Hebrides*, with a description of Johnson's infirmities, and of how he 'was become a little dull of hearing. His sight had always been somewhat weak ... His head, and sometimes also his body, shook with a kind of motion like the effect of a palsy; he appeared to be frequently disturbed by cramps or convulsive contractions, of the nature of that distemper called St. Vitus' dance' (*Journal*, 8). When the pair was storm-bound on the Isle of Skye, a Glasgow newspaper reported that 'such a philosopher, detained on an almost barren island, resembles a whale left upon the strand'. Yet the interest was also a consequence of Johnson's reputed antipathy towards the Scots. Perhaps the most famous of the handful of jokey definitions included in the *Dictionary* was that for Oats, 'A grain, which in England is generally given to horses, but in Scotland supports the people'.[1] The narrator of Johnson's poem, *London*, ironically asks:

> Who would leave, unbribed, Hibernia's land,
> Or change the rocks of Scotland for the Strand?
> There none are swept by sudden fate away,
> But all whom hunger spares, with age decay.

> (*London*, ll. 9–12)

When one of Boswell's reports was reprinted in the *Edinburgh Evening Courant*, the editor appended the observation that 'Dr Johnson is preparing an account of this tour for the press in which the learning, prejudices and pedantry of the celebrated lexicographer will be fully displayed'.

Yet, despite his various widely quoted witticisms at the expense of the Scots, Johnson's trip appears to have been motivated by a desire to experience something of the ancient Highland customs that he felt were being rapidly lost. In part this decline in traditional culture and society was a consequence of the spread of English manners, but it was also the result of a deliberate government policy, following the Highlanders' support for the Stuart monarchy in the Jacobite Risings of 1715 and 1745. After the suppression of the insurrection, penal statutes were passed, forbidding the wearing of Highland dress and the carrying of traditional weapons, and measures were introduced to restrict the use of Erse, the ancient language of the Highlands.

Johnson's *Journey* recounts how these laws have 'operated with efficacy beyond expectation' (*Works*, ix. 90), yet ironically the very success of government action led to a growing intellectual interest in the culture that was being destroyed. As Highland society ceased to be seen as a threat to civilized values, it began to be viewed with nostalgia as an embodiment of a primitive, heroic way of life that could provide a challenge to the corruption identifiable within the modern commercial state. Philosophers in the enlightenment centre of Edinburgh could look up the road to the Highlands to find vestiges of an earlier social system that could be used to substantiate anthropological or sociological theories about the origins of the modern state. The enlightenment historian Adam Ferguson published his *Essay on the History of Civil Society* in 1767, and, one year after the publication of Johnson's work, Adam Smith used his knowledge of the Highlands in his descriptions of primitive economic systems in his *Inquiry into the Nature and Causes of the Wealth of Nations*. In fulfilling his long-held desire to visit the more primitive areas of Scotland, therefore, Johnson was acting in line with a general cultural trend, although he did not share the primitivist belief in the superiority of the lifestyle of the past. Boswell recounts how Johnson engaged in discussion with the primitivist philosopher Lord Monboddo. They 'disputed a little, whether the Savage or the London Shopkeeper had the best existence', with Monboddo arguing for the savage and Johnson the shopkeeper (*Journal*, 56). Perhaps we should not read too much into this debate, since Johnson subsequently admitted that 'he might have taken the side of the savage equally, had anybody else taken the side of the shopkeeper' (*Journal*, 58). But later, when Boswell expressed a belief that mankind was happier in a feudal society than in 'the modern state of independency', Johnson's reply has a ring of sincerity, for it has echoes of the famous letter to Chesterfield. He remarked that:

To be sure, the *Chief* was. But we must think of the number of individuals. That *they* were less happy, seems plain; for that state

81

from which all escape as soon as they can, and to which none return after they have left it, must be less happy; and this is the case with the state of dependence on a chief, or great man. (*Journal, 77*)

Feudal society is associated with that lack of independence that Johnson so resented in his own early life and that he strove so hard to escape.

Given Johnson's renowned sensitivity to the book market, it seems likely that he began his journey with a view to gathering material for some future publication. His translation of Father Lobo's *Voyage to Abyssinia*, as well as *Rasselas*, showed that he had a longstanding interest in the travel-writing genre. Yet in the *Journey* he suggests that the idea for the book came only some weeks into the trip, and Johnson presents a romanticized image of the moment when inspiration struck, while resting the horses in a narrow verdant valley:

I sat down on a bank, such as a writer of Romance might have delighted to feign. I had indeed no trees to whisper over my head, but a clear rivulet streamed at my feet. The day was calm, the air soft, and all was rudeness, silence, and solitude. Before me, and on either side, were high hills, which by hindering the eye from ranging, forced the mind to find entertainment for itself. Whether I spent the hour well I know not; for here I first conceived the thought of this narration.   (Greene, 612)

Yet, despite the pastoral overtones of this passage, the *Journey* does not present a celebration of picturesque landscape in the manner of other tours of the 1770s and 1780s. Compared to Boswell's more effusive *Journal*, there is little appreciation of the dramatic splendour of the wild countryside, which holds scant attraction for Johnson. The hills, we are told:

Exhibit very little variety; being almost wholly covered with dark heath, and even that seems to be checked in its growth. What is not heath is nakedness, a little diversified by now and then a stream rushing down the steep. An eye accustomed to flowery pastures and waving harvests is astonished and repelled by this wide extent of hopeless sterility. The appearance is that of matter incapable of form or usefulness, dismissed by nature from her care and disinherited of her favours, left in its original elemental state, or quickened only with one sullen power of useless vegetation.   (Greene, 611–12)

Because the majority of the land through which Boswell and Johnson travel is regarded as equally sterile and repellent, it is largely passed without comment by Johnson. Likewise, he does not attempt to describe the architecture of the cities he passes through, although these omissions are for rather different reasons. Edinburgh is 'a city too well known to admit description' (Greene, 593), while 'To describe a city so much frequented as *Glasgow* is unnecessary' (*Works*, ix. 159). On the other hand, he does not give an account of Fort George because he cannot 'delineate it scientifically, and a loose and popular description is of use only when the imagination is to be amused' (*Works*, ix. 26). The amusement of the imagination is clearly not seen as Johnson's primary purpose here. We are informed that we cannot be told what sort of commerce was practised by the merchants at Aberdeen, because Johnson did not discover the nature of their business (Greene, 601). In fact, one of the things that first strikes the reader of the *Journey* is the amount of attention Johnson pays to detailing what he is not going to tell us about. His interest is in people rather than places, and the tone of his account is resolutely rational and practical, even when this leads him into areas that he is conscious might be considered too low for a work by such an illustrious hand. His analysis of the design of Scottish windows, and the absence of opening lights, leads him to comment on the consequent smell of Scottish houses. Johnson recognizes that 'these diminutive observations seem to take away something from the dignity of writing', but argues:

> That life consists not of a series of illustrious actions, or elegant enjoyments; the greater part of our time passes in compliance with necessities, in the performance of daily duties, in the removal of small inconveniencies, in the procurement of petty pleasures; and we are well or ill at ease, as the main stream of life glides on smoothly, or is ruffled by small obstacles and frequent interruption. (Greene, 603)

He therefore defends his focus on the ordinary rather than the great on the grounds that:

> The true state of every nation is the state of common life. The manners of a people are not to be found in the schools of learning, or the palaces of greatness, where the national character is

obscured or obliterated by travel and instruction, by philosophy or vanity; nor is happiness to be estimated by the assemblies of the gay, or the banquets of the rich. The great mass of nations is neither rich nor gay: they whose aggregate constitutes the people are found in the streets, and the villages, in the shops and farms; and from them collectively considered, must the measure of general prosperity be taken. (Greene, 603)

His concern is with the manners of the ordinary people, and with estimating public happiness and general prosperity. His work is therefore anthropological and philosophical rather than topographic. This is in line with Johnson's account of the travel writing genre, in *Idler* 97, published on 23 February 1760. In this paper, Johnson argues that 'he that would travel for the entertainment of others, should remember that the great object of remark is human life'. Yet this interest in human life is not purely abstract and cerebral for 'every nation has something peculiar in its manufactures, its works of genius, its medicines, its agriculture, its customs, and its policy. He only is a useful traveller who brings home something by which his country may be benefited; who procures some supply of want or some mitigation of evil'. Far from seeking to amuse the imagination, the aims of the travel writer should be strictly practical. Yet this emphasis on practical observation also has a moral dimension, for knowledge of the condition and polity of others 'may enable his readers to compare their condition with that of others, to improve it whenever it is worse, and whenever it is better to enjoy it' (*Works*, ii. 300).

Johnson's *Journey* is divided into sections, related to the places through which he passed, St Andrews, Aberbrothic, Montrose, Aberdeen, and so on, in the manner of a guide or travel book, but it also starts out as a continuous narrative, following the geographical and chronological progress of the two friends. After their arrival in Ostig in Skye, however, the account loses this narrative focus and becomes increasingly preoccupied with more general philosophical and anthropological issues, as Johnson considers the techniques of Highland agriculture, the character, appearance, and health of the people, their class structure, and the consequence of the legislative attempts to suppress their culture. The narrative moves away from the travel-writing format, to become a more general disquisition in the manner of Ferguson's *Essay on the History of Civil Society*. Yet, while Johnson rejects the primitivist celebration of the culture of the clans, he does not present a simple endorsement of the progressive viewpoint. His ambivalence is evident in his account of Coriatachan in Skye, where he lamented that:

> We came thither too late to see what we expected, a people of peculiar appearance, and a system of antiquated life. The clans retain little now of their original character, their ferocity of temper is softened, their military ardour is extinguished, their dignity of independence is depressed, their contempt of government subdued, and their reverence of their chiefs abated. Of what they had before the late conquest of their country, there remain only their language and their poverty. (Greene, 624)

Robert DeMaria suggests that this sense of belatedness is 'related to his general sense of his own intellectual lateness in the history of literature, imagination, and faith' (DeMaria, 263). He always feels that he has just missed the boat. But such an interpretation implies a respect and nostalgia for the primitive way of life that is not borne out by Johnson's text.

Johnson is able to recognize the virtues of the old clansmen – their courage, hardiness, courtesy, hospitality, and, above, all their loyalty to their chief. He sees some value in the simplicity of Highland life, and admires the ability of the people to cope with an inhospitable climate and environment. But his final verdict is not favourable. The islands, he proclaims, 'have not many allurements but to the mere lover of nature. The inhabitants are thin, provisions are scarce, and desolation and penury give little pleasure' (*Works*, ix. 156). While primitivist writers celebrated the poetic language of the clans that had been handed down from generation to generation, Johnson dismissed the Erse language as 'the rude speech of a barbarous people, who had few thoughts to express, and were content, as they conceived grossly, to be grossly understood' (*Works*, ix. 114). He maintains the suspicion of oral culture that was manifested in both the preface and editorial policy of the *Dictionary*, continuing to emphasize the superiority of the written tradition of an educated public and denigrating the oral vernacular tradition.

The abiding impression he receives from his visit to the Highlands is of a life characterized by hardship and poverty and the romantic appeal of the primitive community is not sufficiently strong to outweigh this view. In accordance with his preoccupation with the practical aspects of travel writing, he outlines areas where improvements could be made in the organization of island life. It is significant that the *Journey* concludes with a passage that is far removed from the issues that have comprised the bulk of the text, as Johnson describes a visit to a school for the deaf in Edinburgh. The success of this project is taken as a symbol of the wider potential for progress, on the grounds that 'having seen the deaf taught arithmetick, who would be afraid to cultivate the *Hebrides*?' (Greene, 641).

Just as *Rasselas* represented a philosophical adaptation of the prose romance, and the *Rambler* provided an intellectual version of the periodical, so the *Journey* can be seen as an attempt to use the popular travel-writing genre to explore issues of moral philosophy, aesthetics, and politics. Johnson uses the incidents and experiences of his tour as stimuli for serious reflections, rather than presenting them as inherently interesting. Even when dealing with issues such as domestic hygiene, which he is conscious may be considered trivial, he does so in terms that highlight the wider intellectual significance of his concern.

The gravity of Johnson's style emerges most clearly when his *Journey* is compared to Boswell's account of the same events in his *Journal of a Tour to the Hebrides*. Johnson's distanced magisterial tone contrasts with Boswell's chatty, anecdotal, and inclusive style. Johnson's anthropological interest in the scenes around him is very different from Boswell's interest in individual stories, and in particular in the character of Johnson himself. From Boswell we get an account of the personal side of the journey – the rows between himself and Johnson, but also the casual conversations and jokes. Boswell transcribes notes and letters he received in the course of the expedition and includes the songs that were sung, the verse that was quoted, and the anecdotes told. You get the impression that he has incorporated everything that he could remember about the trip.

Both writers describe a visit to a Highland hut on the shores of Loch Ness. Johnson gives a detailed account of the appearance of the hut, including its size and mode of construction. He discusses the means of subsistence of the inhabitants, praising their 'true pastoral hospitality' (Greene, 609). He comments that 'To enter a habitation without leave seems to be not considered here as rudeness or intrusion' (Greene, 608), but he makes no mention of the incident described by Boswell as the highlight of the visit:

> Mr Johnson asked me where [the Highland woman] slept. I asked one of the guides, who asked her in Erse. She spoke with a kind of high tone. He told us she was afraid we wanted to go to bed to her. This coquetry, or whatever it may be called, of so wretched a like being, was truly ludicrous. Mr Johnson and I afterwards made merry upon it. I said it was he who alarmed the poor woman's virtue. 'No, Sir', said he 'she'll say, "there came a wicked young fellow, a wild dog, who I believe would have ravished me had there not been with him a grave old gentleman who repressed him" ' . . . 'No', said I. 'She'll say, "There was a terrible ruffian who would have forced me, had it not been for a gentle, mild-looking youth, who, I take it, was an angel." ' (*Journal*, 100)

While Johnson's narrative moves out from the particular incidents to encompass wider speculations and truths, Boswell's account moves inwards to focus on the portrayal of character. The strength of Boswell's writing derives from his presentation of the central character of Johnson and this is explored and celebrated as an extraordinary individual and not as a species. Johnson's concept of characterization in all his varied works looked back to the old neoclassical ideas, but Boswell's portrayal of Johnson looked forward to the mimetic codes of the nineteenth century. Johnson stressed the general, but Boswell was preoccupied with the particular.

In the last years of his life, Johnson became increasingly incapacitated with asthma and kidney failure and in 1783 he suffered a stroke. He managed to recover his faculties, but eventually died on 13 December 1784. He was buried in Westminster Abbey on 20 December, and the following September Boswell's *Journal* appeared. The frankness and explicitness of the work, with its detailed accounts of personal conversations, surprised and shocked many contemporary readers, who had been used to more formal and hagiographic literary lives. But the interest in Johnson was maintained with the publication of William Shaw's anonymous *Memoirs* in 1785, Mrs Piozzi's *Anecdotes* in 1786, Sir John Hawkins's *Life* in 1787, and finally Boswell's *Life* in 1791. Each of these works contributed to the construction of Johnson the idiosyncratic and particular individual.

Within Johnson's own works it has been possible to trace a gradual movement towards a more inclusive concept of the reading public, as he turned his back on the genre of poetic imitation, embraced the vernacular, and sought to make literature accessible to a wider reading public. What he could not accept was the way that this wider reading public would challenge the mimetic codes implicit in traditional literary forms and require a new kind of literature and a new kind of characterization. Despite Johnson's economic dependence on literature, and despite his willingness to explore different literary forms, he did not utilize the genre that was rapidly becoming the most popular and profitable. Johnson never wrote a novel, even though he was an ardent supporter of the work of novel-writing friends such as Samuel Richardson, Charlotte Lennox, and Sarah Fielding. His only play was the classical verse tragedy *Irene*, which had served only to expose the extent of its author's alienation from the requirements of the modern stage.

In trying to establish a link between English literature and the tradition of the classics, Johnson maintained a preoccupation with the general and universal that precluded him from recognizing the increasing importance of the particular and specific. He rejected the intimacy of the novel, with its nuanced morality, in favour of the distanced objectivity of more abstract philosophical discourses with their emphasis on traditional moral precepts. Yet at the same time the extraordinary figure of Johnson emerged from the pages of Boswell, Hawkins, Piozzi, and Shaw as the embodiment of that realistic particularity that he himself sought to repress. As ideas of the role and status of representation changed in the course of the eighteenth century, moving away from classical concepts of character as archetype towards more modern notions of the individual, the great writer became transformed into the great literary subject.

Notes

INTRODUCTION

1. Alvin Kernan, *Printing Technology, Letters and Samuel Johnson* (Princeton: Princeton University Press, 1987), 88.
2. D. G. Greene, *The Politics of Samuel Johnson* (New Haven: Yale University Press, 1960; 2nd edn., Athens, Ga.: University of Georgia Press, 1989).
3. John Cannon, *Samuel Johnson and the Politics of Hanoverian England* (Oxford: Oxford University Press, 1994), 6.
4. J. C. D. Clark, *Samuel Johnson: Literature, Religion and English Cultural Politics from the Restoration to Romanticism* (Cambridge: Cambridge University Press, 1994), 20.
5. Walter Jackson Bate, *The Achievement of Samuel Johnson* (Oxford: Oxford University Press, 1961), 190–1.
6. William Shaw, *Memoirs of the Life and Writings of the Late Dr Samuel Johnson*, repr. with Hester Lynch Piozzi, *Anecdotes of the Late Samuel Johnson, LL.D.*, ed. Arthur Sherbo (London: Oxford University Press, 1974), 11.
7. James T. Boulton (ed.), *Samuel Johnson: The Critical Heritage* (London: Routledge & Kegan Paul, 1971), 21.
8. Ibid. 59.
9. Shaw, *Memoirs*, 27.
10. Lawrence Lipking, *Samuel Johnson: The Life of an Author* (Cambridge, Mass.: Harvard University Press, 2000), 58.

CHAPTER 1. *LONDON* AND *THE VANITY OF HUMAN WISHES*

1. J. C. D. Clark, *Samuel Johnson: Literature, Religion and English Cultural Politics from the Restoration to Romanticism* (Cambridge: Cambridge University Press, 1994), 11.

2. Ibid. 4.
3. Stuart Gillespie, 'A Checklist of Restoration English Translations and Adaptations of Greek and Latin Poetry, 1660–1700', *Translation and Literature*, 1 (1992), 52–67. Cited in Clark, *Samuel Johnson*, 22.
4. John Dryden, 'Preface to the Translation of Ovid's Epistles', in W. P. Ker (ed.), *Essays of John Dryden*, 2 vols. (Oxford, 1926), i. 241.
5. John Dryden, 'Preface to Troilus and Cressida, containing the Grounds of Criticism in Tragedy', in ibid. i. 206.
6. Johnson to Edward Cave, April 1738, in *The Letters of Samuel Johnson*, ed. R. W. Chapman, 3 vols. (1952), i. 16.
7. See also Alvin Kernan, *Printing Technology, Letters and Samuel Johnson* (Princeton: Princeton University Press, 1987), 64.
8. Juvenal, *The Sixteen Satires*, trans. Peter Green (Harmondsworth: Penguin, 1967), Satire III, ll. 273–89.
9. See e.g. T. S. Eliot, 'Johnson as Critic and Poet', in Eliot, *On Poetry and Poets* (London: Faber & Faber, 1971), 162-92.
10. Howard Weinbrot, 'Johnson's Poetry', in Greg Clingham (ed.), *The Cambridge Companion to Samuel Johnson* (Cambridge: Cambridge University Press, 1997), 34–50, at 46.
11. Howard Erskine Hill, 'The Political Character of Samuel Johnson', in Isobel Grundy (ed.), *Samuel Johnson: New Critical Essays* (London: Vision Press, 1984); Clark, *Samuel Johnson*, 142–6.
12. John Cannon, *Samuel Johnson and the Politics of Hanoverian England* (Oxford: Oxford University Press, 1994), 44–8.
13. Lawrence Lipking, *Samuel Johnson: The Life of an Author* (Cambridge, Mass.: Harvard University Press, 2000), 65.
14. Weinbrot, 'Johnson's Poetry', 46.
15. Eccles. 1: 2–3.
16. See Katharine C. Balderston, 'Dr Johnson and William Law', *PMLA* 75 (1960), 382–94.
17. Lipking, *Samuel Johnson*, 86.
18. Weinbrot, 'Johnson's Poetry', 36.
19. Juvenal, *Sixteen Satires*, X, ll. 363–6.
20. See Kernan, *Printing Technology*, but also accounts of Kernan's arguments, which lose some of the nuances: e.g. Thomas Woodman, *A Preface to Samuel Johnson* (London: Longman, 1993), 23.
21. David Nichol Smith, 'Johnson's Poems', in Frederick W. Hilles (ed.), *New Light on Dr Johnson* (New Haven: Yale University Press, 1959), repr. in Donald Greene (ed.), *Samuel Johnson: A Collection of Critical Essays* (Englewood Cliffs, NJ: Prentice-Hall, 1965), 65.
22. Weinbrot, 'Johnson's Poetry', 43.
23. Clark, *Samuel Johnson*, 20.

CHAPTER 2. THE *RAMBLER* AND THE *IDLER*

1. Number 30 was written by Catherine Talbot; 97 by Samuel Richardson; 44 and 100 by Elizabeth Carter. Number 10 contains 4 billets by Hester Mulso. According to Bishop Percy, the second letter in number 15 was written by David Garrick and the second letter in 107 by Joseph Simpson. See D. Nichol Smith, 'The Contributors to *The Rambler* and *The Idler*', *Bodleian Quarterly Record*, 7 [1934], 508–9; W. J. Bate and Albrecht B. Strauss, 'Introduction', in Samuel Johnson, *The Rambler*, ed. W. J. Bate and Albrecht B. Strauss, *Works*, vols. iii–v, p. xxi. References to the *Rambler* not in Greene will be to the Bate and Strauss volumes.
2. Terry Eagleton, *The Function of Criticism, from* The Spectator *to Post-Structuralism* (London: Verso, 1984), 9.
3. Ibid. 10.
4. Eagleton, *Function*, 33.
5. Paul Korshin, 'Johnson, the Essay and *The Rambler*', in Greg Clingham (ed.), *The Cambridge Companion to Samuel Johnson* (Cambridge: Cambridge University Press, 1997), 51–66, at 63.
6. Walter Jackson Bate, *The Achievement of Samuel Johnson* (Oxford: Oxford University Press, 1961), 29.
7. W. K. Wimsatt, *The Prose Style of Samuel Johnson* (New Haven: Yale University Press, 1963), 63.
8. Korshin, 'Johnson, the Essay', 61–2.
9. Liz Bellamy, *Commerce, Morality and the Eighteenth-Century Novel* (Cambridge: Cambridge University Press, 1998), 91.
10. See e.g. Charles Dickens's *Nicholas Nickleby* and *Great Expectations*.
11. Korshin, 'Johnson, the Essay', 55.
12. Bellamy, *Commerce, Morality*, 62–3.
13. Henry Fielding, *The History of Tom Jones*, ed. R. P. C. Mutter (Harmondsworth: Penguin, 1966), 813.
14. Ibid. 853–4.
15. J. C. D. Clark, *Samuel Johnson: Literature, Religion and English Cultural Politics from the Restoration to Romanticism* (Cambridge: Cambridge University Press, 1994), 75.
16. Bate and Strauss, 'Introduction', in *Works*, iii, p. xxxii.
17. Clark, *Samuel Johnson*, 76.

CHAPTER 3. THE *DICTIONARY*

1. J. C. D. Clark, *Samuel Johnson: Literature, Religion and English Cultural Politics from the Restoration to Romanticism* (Cambridge: Cambridge University Press, 1994), 74.

2. Alvin Kernan, *Printing Technology, Letters and Samuel Johnson* (Princeton: Princeton University Press, 1987), 184–5.
3. Allen Reddick, *The Making of Johnson's Dictionary, 1746–1773* (Cambridge: Cambridge University Press, 1996), 1.
4. Sir John Hawkins, *The Life of Samuel Johnson LL.D.* (London, 1787), 345–6.
5. James T. Boulton (ed.), *Samuel Johnson: The Critical Heritage* (London: Routledge & Kegan Paul, 1971), 93.
6. Chesterfield in *The World*, 28 November 1754; Boulton (ed.), *Critical Heritage*, 96–7.
7. Ibid. 104.
8. Ibid.
9. Kernan, *Printing Technology*, 105.
10. Howard Weinbrot, 'Samuel Johnson's *Plan* and Preface to the *Dictionary*: The Growth of a Lexicographer's Mind', in Weinbrot (ed.), *New Aspects of Lexicography* (Carbondale, Ill: Southern Illinois University Press, 1972), 73–94, 87; Reddick, *The Making*, 81.
11. Robert DeMaria, 'Johnson's Dictionary', in Greg Clingham (*ed.*), *The Cambridge Companion to Samuel Johnson* (Cambridge: Cambridge University Press, 1997), 85–101, at 89.
12. Kernan, *Printing Technology*, 200.
13. This term was originally used by Spenser (*Faerie Queene*, iv. ii. 32) in reference to Chaucer, but is used by Johnson to denote the period from the Renaissance to the restoration.
14. John Barrell, *English Literature in History 1730–80* (London: Hutchinson, 1983), 158.
15. DeMaria, 'Johnson's Dictionary', p. 90.
16. Reddick, *The Making*, 121.
17. Ibid., p. xiv.
18. DeMaria, 'Johnson's Dictionary', 124.
19. Reddick, *The Making*, 8.

CHAPTER 4. *RASSELAS*

1. William Hazlitt, *Lectures on the English Comic Writers* (London, 1819), 195–8.
2. See Gwin J. Kolb, 'Introduction', in Samuel Johnson, *Rasselas and Other Tales*, ed. Gwin J. Kolb, *Works*, xvi, pp. xix–xxvi, for an analysis of the different accounts of the writing of the work.
3. Carey McIntosh, *The Choice of Life: Samuel Johnson and the World of Fiction* (New Haven: Yale University Press, 1973), 86.

4. Joseph Addison, *Spectator*, numbers 159, 195, 512, 535, and 631.

5. *Rambler* 38, 65, 120, 190.

6. *Rambler* 204, 205.

7. *Idler*, 75, 99.

8. Cf. *Idler* 186, 187, which contain a story from Greenland.

9. See Percy G. Adams, *Travelers and Travel Liars, 1660–1800* (Berkeley and Los Angeles: University of California Press, 1962).

10. *Rasselas* is reproduced in Greene, 335–418. The quotation is from chapter 1, p. 336. Subsequent references will be included in parentheses in the text and will include chapter number and page reference to Greene.

11. Henry Fielding, *The History of the Adventures of Joseph Andrews and an Apology for the Life of Mrs Shamela Andrews*, ed. Douglas Brooks-Davies (Oxford: Oxford University Press, 1980), book IV, chapter VIII, pp. 276–9.

12. Walter Jackson Bate, *The Achievement of Samuel Johnson* (Oxford: Oxford University Press, 1961), 63–5.

13. Emrys Jones, 'The Artistic Form of *Rasselas*', *Review of English Studies*, NS 18 (1967), 387–401.

14. e.g. John Cannon, *Samuel Johnson and the Politics of Hanoverian England* (Oxford: Oxford University Press, 1994), 131–2.

15. See above, p. 22.

16. Fred Parker, 'The Skepticism of Johnson's *Rasselas*', in Greg Clingham (ed.), *The Cambridge Companion to Samuel Johnson* (Cambridge: Cambridge University Press, 1997), 127–42, 128.

17. Ibid. 127.

18. Voltaire, *Candide, or Optimism*, trans. John Butt (Harmondsworth: Penguin, 1947), 35.

19. Ibid. 144.

20. Ibid.

21. *Critical Review*, 7 (1759), 375.

22. *Monthly Review*, 20 (May 1759), 428–37, repr. in James T. Boulton (ed.), *Samuel Johnson: The Critical Heritage* (London: Routledge & Kegan Paul, 1971), 141–6, at 141.

23. Ibid. 146.

CHAPTER 5. *SHAKESPEARE* AND THE *PREFACES*

1. Terry Eagleton, *The Function of Criticism, from* The Spectator *to Post-Structuralism* (London: Verso, 1984), 29.

2. Cited in James T. Boulton (ed.), *Samuel Johnson: The Critical Heritage* (London: Routledge & Kegan Paul, 1971), 164.

3. Walter Jackson Bate, *The Achievement of Samuel Johnson* (Oxford: Oxford University Press, 1961), 36–9.
4. Cf. Katharine C. Balderstone, 'Johnson's Vile Melancholy', in Frederick W. Hilles (ed.), *The Age of Johnson: Essays Presented to Chauncey Brewster Tinker* (New Haven: Yale University Press, 1949), 3–14.
5. See above, pp. 23–4.
6. William K. Wimsatt, Jr., and Cleanth Brooks, *Literary Criticism: A Short History* (London: Routledge & Kegan Paul, 1957), 320–3; R. D. Stock, *Samuel Johnson and Neoclassical Dramatic Theory* (Lincoln, Neb.: University of Nebraska, 1973).
7. Leopold Damrosch, Jr., *The Uses of Johnson's Criticism* (Charlottesville, Va.: University Press of Virginia, 1976).
8. John D. Boyd, 'Some Limits in Johnson's Literary Criticism', in James Engell (ed.), *Johnson and his Age* (Cambridge, Mass.: Harvard University Press 1984), 192.
9. Henry Fielding, *The History of the Adventures of Joseph Andrews and an Apology for the Life of Mrs Shamela Andrews*, ed. Douglas Brooks-Davies (Oxford: Oxford University Press, 1980), 4.
10. Ibid. 168–9.
11. Ibid. 169.
12. Samuel Johnson, *A Dictionary of the English Language*, 9th edn., 4 vols. (London, 1805), i, unpaginated.
13. Aristotle, *Poetics*, 1451^{a}30–5.
14. Bate, *The Achievement*, 181.
15. e.g. Giles Jacob, Elizabeth Cooper, and Robert Shiels.
16. Bate, *The Achievement*, 185.

CHAPTER 6. *A JOURNEY TO THE WESTERN ISLES*

1. Samuel Johnson, *A Dictionary of the English Language*, 9th edn., 4 vols. (London, 1805), iii, unpaginated.

Select Bibliography

WORKS BY JOHNSON

The Yale Edition of the Works of Samuel Johnson (New Haven: Yale University Press) i. *Diaries, Prayers, and Annals,* ed. E. L. McAdam, Jr., with Donald and Mary Hyde (1958); ii. *The Idler* and *The Adventurer,* ed. W. J. Bate, John M. Bullitt, and L. F. Powell (1963); iii–v. *The Rambler,* ed. W. J. Bate and Albrecht B. Strauss (1969); vi. *Poems,* ed. E. L. McAdam, Jr., with George Milne (1964); vii–viii. *Johnson on Shakespeare,* ed. Arthur Sherbo (1968); ix. *A Journey to the Western Islands of Scotland,* ed. Mary Lascelles (1971); x. *Political Writings,* ed. Donald J. Greene (1977); xiv. *Sermons,* ed. Jean H. Hagstrum and James Gray (1978); xv. *A Voyage to Abyssinia,* ed. Joel J. Gold (1985); xvi. *Rasselas and Other Tales,* ed. Gwin J. Kolb (1990). The most authoritative edition of Johnson's works. The edition should finally run to 24 volumes.

Greene, Donald (ed.), *The Oxford Authors: Samuel Johnson* (Oxford: Oxford University Press, 1984). Contains a good selection of the major poetry and prose.

BIOGRAPHY

Bate, Walter Jackson, *The Achievement of Samuel Johnson* (Oxford: Oxford University Press, 1961). Considers the achievement of Johnson's works through an analysis of his life and beliefs. Now a little dated and superseded by more recent works, which nonetheless owe a considerable debt to Bate.

Boswell, James, *The Life of Samuel Johnson,* ed. R. W. Chapman, rev. J. D. Fleeman, with introduction by Pat Rogers (Oxford: Oxford University Press, 1980). The landmark work that set the standard for subsequent literary biography.

DeMaria, Robert, Jr., *The Life of Samuel Johnson: A Critical Biography* (Oxford: Blackwell, 1993). A succinct account of Johnson's life with thoughtful analysis of the works, emphasizing Johnson's link with European thought.

Hawkins, Sir John, *The Life of Samuel Johnson LL.D.* (London, 1787). Early biography.

Lipking, Lawrence, *Samuel Johnson: The Life of an Author* (Cambridge, Mass.: Harvard University Press, 2000). Explores the life through analysis of the works, with particular reference to the development of the role of the author in eighteenth-century society.

Shaw, William, *Memoirs of the Life and Writings of the Late Dr Samuel Johnson*, and Piozzi, Hester Lynch, *Anecdotes of the Late Samuel Johnson, LL.D.*, ed. Arthur Sherbo (London: Oxford University Press, 1974). Two early biographies of Johnson which form an interesting contrast to Boswell.

CRITICISM

Alkon, Paul, *Samuel Johnson and Moral Discipline* (Evanston, Ill.: Northwestern University Press, 1967). Exploration of Johnson's moral philosophy, now perhaps superseded by Hudson.

Bellamy, Liz, *Commerce, Morality and the Eighteenth-Century Novel* (Cambridge: Cambridge University Press, 1998).

Boulton, James, T. (ed.), *Johnson: The Critical Heritage* (London: Routledge & Kegan Paul, 1971). Useful collection of eighteenth- and nineteenth-century reviews of a range of Johnson's works.

Cannon, John, *Samuel Johnson and the Politics of Hanoverian England* (Oxford: Oxford University Press, 1994). Explores Johnson's ideas in the context of late-twentieth-century ideas of eighteenth-century culture and politics, seeing Johnson as a typical figure of his time, combining radical and reactionary ideas.

Clark, J. C. D., *Samuel Johnson: Literature, Religion and English Cultural Politics from the Restoration to Romanticism* (Cambridge: Cambridge University Press, 1994). Argues against the idea of Johnson as a radical thinker (cf. Greene), representing his thinking as consistently that of a Tory, a Jacobite, and a Nonjuror.

Clingham, Greg (ed.), *The Cambridge Companion to Samuel Johnson* (Cambridge: Cambridge University Press, 1997). An excellent collection of recent studies of Johnson and his works.

Damrosch, Leopold, Jr., *The Uses of Johnson's Criticism* (Charlottesville, Va.: University Press of Virginia, 1976).

Eagleton, Terry, *The Function of Criticism, from* The Spectator *to Post-Structuralism* (London: Verso, 1984),

Engell, James (ed.), *Johnson and his Age* (Cambridge, Mass.: Harvard University Press, 1984). A collection of critical essays on Johnson's life and thought, contemporary developments in literary criticism and the literary, cultural, and historical context of Johnson's work.

Greene, Donald J., *The Politics of Samuel Johnson* (New Haven: Yale University Press, 1960; 2nd edn., Athens, Ga.: University of Georgia Press, 1989). Questions traditional identification of Johnson as a reactionary Tory, and stresses the radicalism of his thought.

—— (ed.), *Samuel Johnson: A Collection of Critical Essays* (Englewood Cliffs, NJ: Prentice-Hall, 1965). Collection of twentieth-century views on Johnson and his work. A bit dated now, but contains some classics of Johnson criticism.

Grundy, Isobel, *Samuel Johnson and the Scale of Greatness* (Leicester: Leicester University Press, 1986). Explores Johnson's work in relation to eighteenth-century ideas of the heroic.

—— (ed.), *Samuel Johnson: New Critical Essays* (London: Vision Press, 1984). A useful collection of critical essays.

Hagstrum, Jean H., *Samuel Johnson's Literary Criticism* (Minneapolis: University of Minnesota Press, 1952). Classic study of Johnson's criticism.

Hart, Kevin, *Samuel Johnson and the Culture of Property* (Cambridge: Cambridge University Press, 1999). Explores the construction of Johnson by his biographers, showing how he was turned into a piece of public property.

Hudson, Nicholas, *Samuel Johnson and Eighteenth-Century Thought* (Oxford: Oxford University Press, 1990). A detailed study of Johnson, setting his moral and religious ideas in the context of the debates within eighteenth-century philosophy.

Kernan, Alvin, *Printing Technology, Letters and Samuel Johnson* (Princeton: Princeton University Press, 1987). Explores the life and work of Johnson in the context of the transition from an oral to a print culture and the change in the role of the author from a gentleman dependent on patronage to the independent professional writer.

McIntosh, Carey, *The Choice of Life: Samuel Johnson and the World of Fiction* (New Haven: Yale University Press, 1973). Analyses and categorizes the prose works that could be described as fiction.

Parker, G. F., *Johnson's Shakespeare* (Oxford: Oxford University Press, 1989). Assesses Johnson's Shakespeare criticism emphasizing its relationship with the plays rather than contemporary critical tradition.

Reddick, Allen, *The Making of Johnson's Dictionary, 1746–1773*, rev. edn. (Cambridge: Cambridge University Press, 1996). Detailed study of the process by which Johnson wrote and subsequently revised the *Dictionary*.

Schwartz, Richard B., *Samuel Johnson and the New Science* (Madison, Wis.: University of Wisconsin Press, 1971). Examines Johnson's thought in relation to Newtonian science.

Tomarken, Edward, *Samuel Johnson: The Discipline of Criticism* (Athens, Ga.: University of Georgia Press, 1991). Explores Johnson's Shakespearian criticism with emphasis on the analysis of the *Notes* as well as the *Preface*.

Wimsatt, William K., Jr., *The Prose Style of Samuel Johnson* (New Haven: Yale University Press, 1941). Detailed analysis of Johnson's style.

—— and Brooks, Cleanth, *Literary Criticism: A Short History* (London: Routledge & Kegan Paul, 1957). Emphasizes neoclassicism of Johnson's critical perspective.

Woodman, Thomas, *A Preface to Samuel Johnson* (London: Longman, 1993). Basic introduction to Johnson describing his life and social, philosophical and political context, providing excerpts from the works with critical analysis.

Index

99

Printed and bound by CPI Group (UK) Ltd, Croydon, CR0 4YY

13/04/2025

14656596-0002